LUTHER AND THE MODERN STATE IN GERMANY

Habent sua fata libelli

Volume VII
of
Sixteenth Century Essays & Studies
James D. Tracy, Editor

This book has been brought to publication with the generous support of
Northeast Missouri State University
and the
University of Minnesota Graduate School

ISBN 0-940474-07-7

Composed by Paula Presley, NMSU, Kirksville, Missouri
Printed by Edwards Brothers, Ann Arbor, Michigan
Text set in Bembo II

LUTHER
AND THE
MODERN STATE
IN GERMANY

James D. Tracy
Editor

Volume VII
Sixteenth Century Essays & Studies

Luther and the modern state in Germany.

(Sixteenth century essays & studies; v. 7)
Includes bibliographical references and index.
1. Luther, Martin, 1483-1546–Influence.
2. Political science–History. 3. Germany–Politics and
government. I. Tracy, James D. II. Series.
BR333.5.P6L87 1986   320.1'092'4   86-20400
ISBN 0-940474-07-7

TABLE OF CONTENTS

Acknowledgements

Three of the essays appearing here (those by Schilling, Brady, and Gritsch) were first presented as papers at a conference on "Luther and the City of Man" at the University of Minnesota in November 1983, organized by Gerhard Weiss (German Department) and myself. Heinz Schilling's "Lutherjahr" lecture tour of the United Sates was made possible by the German Federal Republic, while the Minnesota Humanities Commission provided major support for our conference at Minnesota. Thomas Brady provided the translation of Karlheinz Blaschke's article that appears here, collaborated in the translation of Professor Schilling's essay, and made helpful suggestions for my own Introduction. Brent Peterson's paper was first read at the Sixteenth Century Studies Conference in 1984. Publication of this volume of Sixteenth Century Essays & Studies was made possible by a grant from the University of Minnesota graduate school. Three units of the College of Liberal Arts–the Department of History, the Office of Research and Development, and the West European Area Studies Center–provided additional support both for the 1983 conference and for this volume.

J. D. T.

Luther and the Modern State:
Introduction to A Neuralgic Theme

James D. Tracy
University of Minnesota

THIS VOLUME ADDRESSES A TOPIC WHICH, though often the object of ambushes and flank attacks from several scholarly directions, is seldom assaulted head-on. Five scholars discuss connections between Luther and the development of the modern state in Germany from two different angles. For some, the principal question is whether there is in fact a discernible relationship between what Luther taught and the subsequent growth of princely absolutism in Germany. For others, there is a further issue as to how Luther has been and is understood by those who invoke his teaching in order to legitimize a particular conception of the state.

Apart from those who may have a personal or professional interest in Luther's doctrines, it is still commonly believed among educated people that Luther was a prophet of authoritarian government. Willliam Shirer's brief allusions to Luther in his *Rise and Fall of the Third Reich*[1] are less a cause of this widespread perception than an indication of it. In this case, as often happens, popular opinion is a fairly accurate reflection of the conclusions reached by scholars of a previous generation. One of the great monuments of *Geistesgeschichte*, or intellectual history in the German manner, is *The Social Teachings of the Christian Churches* by Ernst Troeltsch (d. 1923), who contrasted unfavorably the conservative, even reactionary tendencies of Lutheranism with the dynamism of the Calvinist movement.[2] There is also an Anglo-American scholarly tradition, aware of but not really shaped by works in the German language, in which Luther figures as a foil to those scholastic and Enlightenment thinkers who, it is argued, created the intellectual foundations for democratic government.

In 1941 William Montgomery McGovern, a political scientist at Northwestern and sometime lecturer at Harvard, published a lengthy study entitled *From Luther to Hitler; the History of Fascist-Nazi Political Philosophy*. At a time when most Americans were still resolved not to enter the war in Europe, McGovern presented England and America as the last champions of liberalism, and the last barriers to worldwide triumph of fascism. Should a democratic

[1]Shirer, *Rise and Fall of the Third Reich* (New York: Simon & Schuster, 1960), 91, 236.

[2]Troeltsch, *The Social Teachings of the Christian Churches*, tr. Olive Wyon, 2 vols. (New York: Harper, 1960).

power be "forced to enter into armed conflict with a totalitarian power," wrote McGovern, it would be essential to have full information about enemy armaments. "In like manner, in the ideological conflict between liberalism and fascism (and such a conflict is already under way)," liberals must be armed with knowledge of the "types of arguments which are used by Fascists to win converts to their cause." Although McGovern supplied Fascism with an intellectual pedigree tracing back to Plato's *Republic*, he chose to begin his discussion with the Reformation, which enhanced state power by breaking down the universal church, and which ended, even in Catholic lands, by subjugating the church to the state.[3]

While he was not explicit on this point, McGovern seemed to give liberalism too ancient a lineage, since he described it as being "on the wane" in early seventeenth-century England, prior to the civil war. One may infer that McGovern shared in the regnant view of the evolution of western political thought in which—to quote J. N. Figgis, who in turn quoted Lord Acton—"St. Thomas Aquinas was the first Whig."[4] Many English and American scholars of this era regarded the democratic liberties of the twentieth century as the fortunate result of political institutions and political ideas that had roots in medieval England. This whole outlook, though subjected to a very effective critique in Herbert Butterfield's essay, *The Whig Interpretation of History* (1931), continued to flourish on into the 1940s.[5]

In a curious way, Anglo-American belief in England's peculiar destiny mirrors and complements an opposing German conception as reflected in a 1922 essay by Ernst Troeltsch.[6] Both sides agreed that the fundamental question in political thought had to do with the moral foundation of the state. Should the state be regarded as having been created by a compact among its citizens, reflecting certain universal principles of natural law? Or should each state rather be seen as the organic product of a distinct historical development, generating its own unique ethical norms? Both sides agreed further that the former view was characteristically "western," tracing from scholastic theories of natural law and the social contract through John Locke and the French Enlightenment, and the latter view was a specific creation of German Roman-

---

[3]McGovern, *From Luther to Hitler: The History of Fascist Political Philosophy* (Cambridge, Mass.: Houghton, Mifflin, 1941). Chapt. 1, "The Liberal and Fascist Traditions," 3-17; also 21.

[4]McGovern, *From Luther to Hitler*, 80; J. N. Figgis, *Studies in Political Thought from Gerson to Gotius, 1414-1625* (London: Cambridge University Press, 1907), 7-8.

[5]Butterfield, *The Whig Interpretation of History* (London: G. Bell, 1931).

[6]Troeltsch, "The Ideas of Natural Law and Humanity in World Politics," in Otto Gierke, *Natural Law and the Theory of Society*, tr. Ernest Barker (Reprint of 1934 edition; Cambridge: Cambridge University Press, 1958), 201-22, with Barker's Introduction, xv-xviii, xliv-xlvi, l-liv, lvii-lxiv.

ticism and its defense of the collective individuality of peoples, as against the abstract universalism of the Englightenment.[7]

It seems easy enough now to recognize that both the Anglo-American and the German interpretations of European intellectual history expressed the aspirations and fears of great nations pitted against each other in mortal combat. At a distance of forty-five years, one can well honor McGovern as a democrat in democracy's hour of need, even while recognizing that his book lacks the enduring qualities of good scholarship. The real problem lies not so much in his personal bias as in the presuppositions of *Geistesgeschichte* as a way of understanding the past, practiced by scholars as diverse as Troeltsch and Figgis.[8] For if one assumes that ideas "unfold" or work out their consequences over time in direct fashion, it may well seem logical to conclude that bad government, or evil policy, must be traceable back to wrong-headed ideas of one sort or another. One arrives, in effect, at a secular version of the ancient ecclesiastical prejudice, according to which false doctrine will inevitably manifest itself in immoral behavior. The odd thing is that although *Geistesgeschichte* of this sort often bows to Hegel, it is bad Hegelianism, for Hegel himself never envisioned a direct or linear development of the logical possibilities of a given idea. Historians of the inter-war years, without becoming Hegelians themselves, were certainly familiar with the idea that historical development can better be understood as a dialectical process than as a linear progress. For example, it was commonly argued that absolute monarchy, far from suppressing individual liberty, curtailed "liberties" in the medieval sense—that is, noble and ecclesiastical privileges—and so paved the way for the eventual triumph of equality before the law.[9] If some writers treated Romanticism as a characteristically German aberration of the mind, leading by dark paths toward National Socialism,[10] Jacques Barzun's *Romanticism and the Modern Ego* (1943) demonstrated that Romanticism was a European current of thought, and that its political implications were to be seen not in totalitarian movements, but in the democratic principle of national self-determination.[11]

[7]For more recent versions of this argument, see Leonard Krieger, *The German Idea of Freedom* (Boston: Beacon, 1957); and George G. Iggers, *The German Conception of History* (Middletown, Conn.: Wesleyan University Press, 1968).

[8]Figgis, *Studies in Political Thought*, 2: "Hildebrand, Calvin and Rousseau were doctrinaires, if ever there were such. Yet neither Bismarck, nor even Napoleon, has had a more terrific strength to shape the destinies of man." As Jacques Barzun has said, "the libraries are full of books usually written in wartime, and which show that from Luther to Hitler, or from Fichte to Mussolini, or from Rousseau to Stalin 'one increasing purpose runs' ": *Classic, Romantic, and Modern* , (Boston, 1961), 9 (revision of *Romanticism and the Modern Ego* [1943]).

[9]A. J. Slavin, ed. *The New Monarchies and Representative Assemblies* (Boston: Heath, 1965); for a more recent and quite different view, Perry Anderson, *Lineages of the Absolutist State* (London: N.L.B., 1979).

[10]See the chapter on Romanticism in Peter Viereck, *Metapolitics: From the Romantics of Hitler* (New York: Knopf, 1941), 16-47.

[11]See above, note 8.

But Germany is a special case; the historical imagination has difficulty accepting the possibility that there are adequate short-term explanations for the phenomenon of National Socialism. Hence one will still find defenders of the proposition that Germany's distinctive intellectual and political development over the centuries (*der deutsche Sonderweg*) was somehow irretrievably warped, pointing the way for Adolf Hitler. Arguments of this nature focus on such things as the tradition of bureaucratic absolutism in Germany's princely states,[12] or on the allegedly baneful influence of German idealism, with its high conception of the state as a moral community.[13] Luther figures in the background on both counts, as a champion of princely authority, and as a thinker of "irrationalist" leanings, whose murky lucubrations make him a precursor of German idealism.[14]

In the end, it is simply not possible to disentangle Luther's place in German history from broader issues concerning the character of Germany's historical development. One cannot think of German history without Luther, any more than without Goethe or Bismarck. Such is the message of Thomas Mann's essay "Die Drei Gewaltigen" (1949), in which Luther, the earliest of the three "powerful ones" who have shaped Germany's destiny, is presented as "a primitive, but deeply spiritual, inwardly oriented eruption of the German nature . . . a powerful hater, ready heart and soul for bloodletting." The great novelist's attitude toward Luther is in one sense instructive. Without changing his perception of Luther as the man who set Germany on a path of development different from that of western Europe—notably in his rejection of the humanist outlook—Mann moves from a favorable judgment of Luther (*Betrachtungen eines Unpolitischen*, 1918) to one that is quite hostile, precisely because National Socialism had invested the idea of Germany's "special path" with new and sinister meaning.[15] Setting such large issues to one side, this

---

[12]Hans Rosenberg, *Bureaucracy, Aristocracy, Autocracy: The Prussian Experience, 1660-1815* (Boston: Beacon, 1958).

[13]See the sections on Hegel in Viereck, *Metapolitics*, 199-23, and Bertrand Russell, *A History of Western Philosophy* (New York: Simon & Schuster, 1945), 730-46. As for Luther, Viereck, 13, acknowledges that he was "more aroused by Christian than by nationalist motives. Yet as a popular movement the German Reformation was a nationalist *Kultur* ousting as alien the Renaissance and humanism, those superb flowers of Mediterranean and western civilization."

[14]Rosenberg, *Bureaucracy, Aristocracy, Autocracy*, 22, speaks of the "political docility and social quietism of orthodox Lutheranism." Otto Hintze, "Calvinism and Raison d'Etat in Seventeenth Century Brandenburg," in *The Historical Essays of Otto Hintze*, ed. Felix Gilbert (New York, 1975), 88-154, presents Lutheranism, in contrast to Calvinism, as clinging to the past, in a manner that reflects the social and political backwardness of the territories from which it sprang. Igggers, *The German Conception of History*, 33, agrees with Troeltsch that "in place of the concept of a rational law of nature, Luther substituted an irrational law of nature."

[15]Mann, "Die Drei Gewaltigen," in *Gesammelte Werke* (Oldenberg: Fischer, 1960), xx, 374-83, here 375-76, "ein roher, dabei tief beseelter und inniger ausbruch deutscher Natur . . . ein mächtiger Hasser, zum Blutvergiessen von ganzem Herzen bereit." Contrast *Reflections of an Unpolitical Man*, tr. Walter D. Morris (New York: Ungar, 1983), Chapter 10, "On Belief," esp. 376-95.

volume will deal with specific questions about Luther, which are complicated enough in themselves. But readers are forewarned that the sixteenth-century salvos touched off here are but the rattle of an arquebus as compared with the running thunder of modern artillery just over the horizon.

*   *   *

Given McGovern's title, one would expect more than the few pages he actually devoted to Luther. McGovern classed him among the precursors of Fascism because he preached a supine obedience to princes, and prided himself for so doing, and because his movement reduced the church to princely control, thus removing an important obstacle to the growth of an all-powerful state. Among the secondary accounts of Luther that he used, McGovern favored the interpretation of J. N. Figgis (1907), rather than the more nuanced views of J. W. Allen (1928).[16] But in 1941 it would not have been easy to find serious scholarship that did not interpret the tendency of Luther's thought as hostile to individualism and democracy. James Mackinnon's *Luther and the Reformation* (4 vols., 1925-1930), which remains even today the lengthiest English-language biography, distinguishes again and again between the young Luther's inestimable service to the principles of liberty, and the betrayal of these principles by a somewhat older Luther railing against rebel peasants or rabid sectarians: "In the end, Protestantism was a bigger thing than its sixteenth-century creator could grasp. It involved the fact of progress."[17] As for German scholarship, one of the few works available in English was Troeltsch's *Social Teachings* (translated in 1931), with its picture of a Lutheranism sunk in authoritarian lethargy. Finally, as Thomas Brady shows here, the Luther Renaissance in Germany included not a few scholars who had reasons of their own for presenting Luther as schoolmaster of the German people in the discipline of obedience (*Gehorsamkeit*).

Merely to contemplate this tradition of interpretation is to recognize at once that it belongs to a different, bygone world. Already in the 1940s, as Eric Gritsch points out, the crimes of National Socialism compelled dissident Protestant movements in Norway and Germany to rediscover a Luther very different from the national hero celebrated by those who called themselves

---

[16]McGovern, *From Luther to Hitler*, 30-35, 48; J. W. Allen, *A History of Political Thought in the Sixteenth Century* (reprint of 1928 edition; London: Methuen, 1960), 29: "'Had there been no Luther there could never have been a Louis XIV.' The well-known epigram of Dr. Figgis seems to have no relation to fact." The reference is to Figgis, *Studies in Political Thought*, 71.

[17]Mackinnon, *Luther and the Reformation*, 4 vols. (New York: Longmans, Green, 1925-1930), vol. 4, p. 335.

"German Christians." Troeltsch's views about the dead weight of a Lutheran heritage are difficult to take too seriously if one considers the pioneering role of the Scandinavian countries in the development of the welfare state, or, closer to home, the progressive political tradition of America's northern prairie states, which have large Lutheran populations. If Luther studies are just now beginning to flourish in the German Democratic Republic, it is partly because, as Brent Peterson suggests, a state grown more secure in the sense of its own legitimacy can also be more confident about reclaiming its "heritage."

At the same time, new directions of investigation within the historical profession have reshaped the framework in which scholars ask questions about Luther. Brent Peterson's description of how a new understanding of Luther has grown out of the Leipzig work group for the Early Bourgeois Revolution shows how the concentration of intellectual resources on a chosen topic can produce unexpected results. Readers of this volume need not be reminded that both the Sixteenth Century Studies Conference and the American Society for Reformation Research were organized within fifteen years of the end of World War II.

Several important developments within the broader context of the study of European history bear directly on the Reformation. First, the traditional distinction between academic history and local, usually amateur, history has been broken down by the movement toward technically proficient, generalizing studies in local history. This work has been pioneered in France by the *Annales* school, and in Germany, where local history was always more respectable, by Otto Brunner and his disciples. The premise of such works, stated or not, is that a narrower geographical focus makes it possible to study the development over time of an identifiable society, and thus to gain a more rounded picture of the past than is afforded by the study of great events on the national or international stage. Studies of the urban Reformation, especially after the stimulus provided by Bernd Moeller's *Reichsstadt und Reformation* (1962), are only the most obvious fruit of the pursuit of local history in sixteenth-century Germany. Studies of princely territories, including those by Heinz Schilling and Karlheinz Blaschke,[18] are another. One implication of these works is that "the Reformation" is best understood not as a political epoch that ended with the Peace of Augsburg (1555)—though some still defend this view—but rather as a broad movement for the reform of Christian society, whose specific goals

---

[18]Blaschke, *Sachsen im Zeitalter der Reformation*, Schriften des vereins für Reformationsgeschichte (Gütersloh: Mohn, 1970), 185; Volker Press, *Calvinismus und Territorialstaat: Regierung und Zentralbehörden der Kurpfalz, 1559-1619* (Stuttgart: Klett, 1968); Schilling, *Konfessionskonflikt und Staatsbildung: eine Fallstudie über das Verhältnis von religiösem und socialem Wandel in der Frühneuzeit am beispiel der Grafschaft Lippe*, Vol. 48 of *Quellen und Forschungen zur Reformationsgeschichte* (Gütersloh: Mohn, 1981).

zealous clerics and bureaucrats were still pursuing late into the seventeenth century.[19]

Secondly, the venerable distinction between sacred and profane history is disappearing. It may well be, as Heinz Schilling suggests elsewhere, that the union of these previously separate research orientations has been rather one-sided in practice, yielding more studies of the secular dimensions of religious history than of the religious dimensions of secular history.[20] Nonetheless, the process by which Marxist scholars have come to recognize theology as an autonomous sphere of human endeavor, documented here for East German Luther studies by Brent Peterson, can only be described as remarkable. In the United States and western Europe, the way in which the concept of Renaissance humanism has acquired a religious content that it almost totally lacked a generation ago is only slightly less remarkable. The confluence of Renaissance and Reformation as a common field of study can be seen superficially in "Ren-Ref" job listings over the last three decades or so, and more profoundly in the work of scholars like Charles Trinkaus and William J. Bouwsma. Meanwhile, students of Reformation religious thought show more interest in questions of social and political context, and less in the methods of *Geistesgeschichte*, in which, rather as in textbooks for systematic theology, a Reformer's theology became a deductive chain of compartments, each containing the *Lehre* appropriate to that topic.

To take an example especially pertinent here, Hans-Joachim Gaenssler and Eike Wohlgast, authors of the most recent monographs on Luther's political ideas, do not find in his writings a coherent *Zwei-Reichen Lehre*. Rather, they show him responding to different contingencies as occasion required, so that even his treatise *Von Weltlicher Obrigkeit* (1523) reflects a variety of concrete concerns that are not easily composed into a single perspective. At the one point where political issues touch most directly on Luther's cardinal theological doctrine, he reaches a conclusion not palatable to princes—namely, that the prince has no right to coerce the consciences of his subjects[21] It was precisely at this point, according to James Estes, that the theologian-architects of Lutheran state churches, like Johannes Brenz, found Luther's thought in

---

[19]Contrast Schilling's conception of the confessional age in European history, *Konfessionskonflikt und Statsbildung*, 23-26, with Blaschke's remark in *Sachsen im Zeitalter der Reformation*, 114, that the Reformation "zog sich als bewegung über einen Zeitraum von etwa 40 Jahren hin."

[20]Schilling, *Konfessionskonflikt und Staatsbildung*, 15-17.

[21]Hans Joachim Gaenssler, *Evangelium und weltliches Schwert: Hintergrund, Entstehungsgeschichte, und Anlass von Luthers Scheidung zweier Reiche oder Regimente*, Veröffentlichungen des Instituts für europäische Geschichte Mainz, Abteilung für abendlandische Religionsgeschichte (Wiesbaden: Steiner, 1983), 109; Eike Wohlgast, *Die wittenberger Theologie und die Politik der evangelischen Stände: Studien zu Luthers Gutachten in politischen Fragen*, Vol. 47 of *Quellen und Forschungen zur Reformationsgeschichte* (Gütersloh: Mohn, 1977). Gunther Wolf, ed., *Luther und die Obrigkeit*, Vol. 85 of *Wege der Forschung* (Darmstadt: Wissenschaftliche Buchgesellschaft, 1972) presents excerpts from scholarship of the 1950s and 1960s.

need of correction. Since Luther encouraged princes to suppress false worship, lest the wrath of God be provoked, it was "illogical" for the prince not to employ his full power to establish true worship, and to compel his subjects to conform to it.[22]

Finally, one can see in recent studies the possibility of a third important step, which no scholar has yet taken. Here and elsewhere, Heinz Schilling makes a compelling argument that "confessionalization" is a recognizable historical process that is broadly comparable across the major lines of religious division in Europe. If the formation of state churches is more a defining characteristic for the history of Germany than for other countries during the same period, it is because the Empire's political fragmentation permitted the establishment of three different confessional traditions, often side by side, rather than a single national church.[23] In principle, then, one ought to be able to learn a great deal about religion and society in early modern Europe by comparing the adjacent state churches of two different confessions. In actuality, comparative studies of this kind are still quite rare,[24] although we already have in hand adequate methods for gauging the effects of state-church regulation on the religious and moral behavior of the common people, thanks to the pioneering studies of Gabriel Le Bras and his disciples on the Counter-Reformation in seventeenth-century French dioceses. Decanal visitation records (much more reliable than episcopal reports) have been used to good effect for the Spanish Netherlands by Michel Cloet and others, while Heinz Schilling and A. Th. van Deursen have shown the value of consistorial protocols for religious life in the Calvinist Dutch Republic. For Germany, Gerald Strauss and James Kittelson have opened up Lutheran visitation records as a source for the same topic.[25]

[22]James Martin Estes, *Christian Magistrate and State Church: The Reforming Career of Johannes Brenz* (Toronto: University of Toronto Press, 1982), 33ff.

[23]Schilling, *Konfessionskonflikt und Staatsbildung,* 23-34.

[24]Peter Zschunke, *Konfession und Alltag in Oppenheim: Beiträge zur Geschichte von Bevölkerung und Gesellschaft einer gemischtkonfessionellen Kleinstadt der frühen Neuzeit,* Veröffentlichungen des Instituts für europäische Geschichte Mainz, Abteilung für abendländische religionsgeschichte (Wiesbaden: Steiner, 1984), 115; Benjamin Kaplan, a student of Steven Ozment at Harvard, is at work on a dissertation comparing the religious life of Calvinist and Catholic communities in the Dutch province of Utrecht. For a comparative overview of scholarly literature, with some reference to the Calvinist Hervormde Kerk, see Tracy, "With and without the Counter-Reformation: the Catholic Church in the Spanish Netherlands and the Dutch Republic, 1570-1650," *Catholic Historical Review* 71 (1985): 547-75.

[25]Gabriel Le Bras, *Etudes de sociologie religieuse,* 2 vols. (Paris: Presses Universitaires de France, 1955); Jeanne Ferté, *La vie Religieuse dans les Campagnes Parisiennes, 1622-1695* (Paris, 1964); Robert Sauzet, *Contre-Reforme et reforme Catholique en bas Languedoc* (Brussels: Nauwelaerts, 1979); Michel Cloet, *Het Kerkelijk Leven in een Landelijk Dekenij van Vlaanderen: Thielt van 1609 tot 1700* (Louvain:: Universiteitsbibliotheek, 1968); Th. B. Kok, *Dekanat in de Steigers: Kerkelijk Opbouwwerk in het Gentse Dekanat Hulst, 1596-1648* (Tilburg: Stichting Zuidelijk Historisch Contact, 1971); Heinz Schilling, "Religion und Gesellschaft in der calvinistischen Republik der Niederlande," in Franz Petri, ed., *Kirche und gesellschaftlicher Wandel in deutschen und niederländischen Städten der werdenden Neuzeit,* Veröffentlichungen des Instituts für vergleichende Städteforschung

One who samples this growing literature will find it hard to credit the argument that the whole phenomenon of state-church regimentation is traceable to any specific doctrines of Martin Luther. It is true that the church enjoyed both in Catholic and Calvinist territories a formal independence that had no counterpart in Lutheran Germany. Lay Catholic princes often had to contend with bishops or abbots who were themselves princes of the Empire, while the presence of lay elders in Calvinist consistories marked the continuance in some measure of the principle of communal government. But differences of ecclesiastical polity did not necessarily affect the degree to which the lives of ordinary folk were subjected to official control. Strauss finds that Calvinist rulers were more inclined to resort to "strong-armed" methods, such as having constables patrol the streets during hours of Sunday service to gather in strays; Schilling points out that lay elders were sometimes appointed by the prince, rather than elected from the congregations, and so became minor bureaucrats.[26] Habsburg Tyrol included within its boundaries two ecclesiastical principalities, Brixen and Trent, whose prince-bishops struggled constantly and with some success to maintain their independence. But, save for indulging the inveterate Protestant tendencies of miners in the Inntal, the Archduke's officials deployed a religious *Policey* that would have been the envy of most Protestant functionaries, including "book visitations" to enforce censorship, and annual "confession certificates" for Tyrolean subjects who earned their bread in Protestant lands.[27] If a "liberal" after the manner of William McGovern could somehow be transported back into the seventeenth-century Empire, it is by no means clear he would find life more palatable in a Calvinist or a Catholic territory than in a Lutheran one.

The question of Luther's role in the formation of territorial churches thus merges into a larger question about the confluence of religious reform movements and the growing power of the state. Carrying his inquiry forward to

in Münster, Darstellung 10 (Vienna/Cologne: Bohlau, 1980), 198-250; and "Reformierte Kirchenzucht als soziale Disziplinierung? Die Tätigkeit des emdener Presbyteriums in den Jahren 1557-1662," in Wilfried Ehbrecht, Heinz Schilling, eds., *Niederlande und Nordwestdeutschland: Studien zur regional- und Stadtgeschichte Nordwestkontinentaleuropas im Mittelalter und in der Neuzeit Franz Petri zum 80en Geburtstag* (Vienna/Cologne: Bohlau, 1983), 261-327; A. Th. van Deursen, *Bavianen en Slijkgeuzen: Kerk en Kerkvolk tenn Tijde van Maurits en Oldenbarnevelt* (Assen; van Gorcum, 1979), Chapt. 9, "Christelijke Zeden en Levenstucht," 193-216; Gerald Strauss, *Luther's House of Learning* (Baltimore: Johns Hopkins University Press, 1978); and James Kittelson, "Success or Failure of the Reformation: A Report from Strasbourg," *Archiv für Reformationsgeschichte* 73 (1983): 153-74.

[26]Schilling, *Konfessionskonflikt und Staatsbildung*, 189; by way of contrast, see Schilling, "Calvinistischen Presbyterien in Städten der Frühneuzeit—eine kirchliche alternativform zur bürgerlichen Repräsentation?" in Wilfried Ehbrecht, ed., *Städtische Führungsgruppen und Gemeinde in der werdenden Neuzeit*, Veroffentlichungen des Instituts für vergelichende Städteforschung in Münster, Darstellung 9 (Vienna/Cologne: Bohlau, 1980), 385-444.

[27]Jürgen Bücking, *Frühabsolutismus und Kirchenreform in Tirol (1566-1665): ein Beitrag zum Ringen zwischen "Staat" und "Kirche" in der frühen Neuzeit*, Vol. 66 of *Veroffentlichungen des Institut für europäische Geschichte Mainz, Abteilung für abendländische Religionsgeschichte* (Wiesbaden: Steiner, 1972), 63-98, 126-41, 175-89.

1620, Strauss finds little reason for believing that Lutheran reformers were successful in their aim of creating a truly Christian society, and it is hard to imagine that much could have been done in the building of religious communities during the Thirty Years' War. Yet studies of the Counter-Reformation, often carried farther into the seventeenth century, suggest that the constant application of pressure from zealous preachers and officious bureaucrats, "like water dropping on a stone," gradually did change people's attitudes towards such things as receiving the sacraments, sending children to catechism classes, and even abstaining from sexual intercourse prior to marriage.[28] Changes of this kind did not take effect without the active cooperation of the state and its police powers, the efficacy of which Strauss himself seems willing to grant. It seems likely, then, that only the curious dearth of studies of religious life in seventeenth-century German territories prevents one from concluding that Lutheran state churches sooner or later achieved comparable results. As studies of this kind are carried out, it is possible they may disclose a pattern of regimentation that was somewhat stricter in German-speaking lands than in other parts of Europe. The Calvinist church of the Netherlands, constantly at loggerheads with "libertine" magistrates in the towns, was never able to back up its decrees with the kind of "strong-armed" methods that some German Calvinist princes employed.[29] Similarly, one has the impression that Habsburg Catholicism was rather more heavy-handed in Tyrol than in the Spanish Netherlands, where the custom of Protestant merchants was welcome, and where towns and provincial assemblies still had vestiges of their former autonomy.[30]

Supposing for the moment that Lutheran state churches did achieve an outward religious conformity that bore some resemblance to the godly community that most reformers had desired, there remains the question of what significance one attaches to such a transformation. Gerald Strauss is of the opinion that attitudes imposed from above, rather than freely embraced, cannot long endure. Similarly, historians of seventeenth-century Catholic lands sometimes remark, with evident distaste, on the timid and obsequious character of Counter-Reformation religion.[31] Yet one wonders whether such

---

[28]Tracy, "With and Without the Counter-Reformation," 554-59; cf. Bücking, *Frühabsolutismus und Kirchenreform in Tirol*, 73: "Obwohl von den angedrohten Strafen nur in Ausnahmefällen (z. B. in Verbindung mit anderen Vergehen) Gebrauch gemacht wurde, wirkten diese ständigen gedruckten Mandaten wie der sprichwörterliche stete Tropfen auf den Stein."

[29]R. B. Evenhuis, *Ook Dat Was Amsterdam*, 3 vols. (Amsterdam: Ten Haue, 1965-1971), Vol. 2, 113-32.

[30]Compare Bücking, *Frühabsolutismus und Kirchenreform in Tirol*, with Cloet, *Het Kerkelijk Leven in een Landelijke Dekenij van Vlaanderen*, and Kok, *Dekenat in de Steigers*.

[31]Strauss, *Luther's House of Learning*, 299; "Drill promoted resentment and opposition, boredom and apathy. By and large this seems to have been the end product of religious indoctrination." Kok, *Dekenat in de Steigers*, characterizes the clerical mentality of the seventeenth century as "pastoral theology reduced to commands and prohibitions, like barbed wire round the sheep pen."

views do not amount to a Whig interpretation of religious history, according to which the growth of moral consciousness is the product only of individual choices, and never of coercive authority. Jean Delumeau comments at one point that it took a thousand years of Christian preaching to create a sense of individual responsibility, absent among the Greeks but evident in the Renaissance.[32] If this be true, might it not also be the case that the Enlightenment's easy confidence in the moral goodness of human nature depended on some 150 years of precisely the kind of guilt-ridden religion which the *philosophes* themselves so despised?

In this debate between church order and individual liberty, Martin Luther is the only religious thinker of his era who can be invoked with equal justice on both sides. An independent Protestant of the Reformed tradition would never think of appealing to Calvin against dominees eager to marshall state power in the service of the orthodoxy, any more than a zealous Counter-Reformation Catholic would call upon Erasmus in support of the Inquisition, or the Index of Forbidden Books. Yet it was perfectly reasonable for eighteenth-century Pietists to summon Luther himself to bear witness against the Lutheran orthodoxy that had been so carefully erected on the foundations of his theology. Precisely because he embraced within himself the claims of liberty and order, stated cogently and acutely in each case, Luther never gives the impression of being a one-dimensional thinker, and he always repays the effort of further study. It is in that spirit that this present volume is conceived.

Cf. Bücking, *Frühabsolutismus und Kirchenreform in Tirol*, 175: "Die Bemühungen um die äussere und innere Restitution erreichten in dieser Phase ihren Hohepunkt, und begrundete jene ängstliche, sich verschliessende Katholizität, der Tirol seinen Weltruf als streng Katholisches Land verdankt."

[32]Delumeau, *Catholicism between Luther and Voltaire*, tr. Jeremy Meiser (London, 1977), 170.

The Reformation and the Rise of the Early Modern State

Heinz Schilling
University of Giessen
Translated by Heinz Schilling and Thomas A. Brady, Jr.

THE RELATIONSHIP BETWEEN THE REFORMATION and the rise of the early modern state seems a very traditional theme. One might be tempted, following current wisdom, to sum it up with the phrases, "Luther and the authoritarian German state" or "the servile mentality of the German Lutherans." Since World War II in particular, there has existed a widespread notion of a direct connection between Luther and Adolf Hitler, and the general public tends to believe that, despite possible exaggerations, there is some truth in the notion. Luther and his theology appear as essential elements in the German divergence from western European history, what some historians call "the German path."[1] The 500th anniversary of Luther's birth provides an opportunity to ask whether there was in fact a logical or historical connection between Luther and the authoritarian state (Obrigkeitsstaat).

Let me state my own position at the outset: public opinion is wrong in blaming Luther and the Lutheran Reformation for the faults of German political life in the nineteenth and twentieth centuries. The position of some historians and sociologists–that the influence of Luther and Lutheranism on early modern political development was fundamentally different from those of Calvin or Calvinism or of the popes and Catholicism–is unacceptable. This analysis will assume a broader than normal context, for Lutheranism and German state building will be set in a framework of confessionalization and state building as universal phenomena of early modern Europe. Also described will be the uniquely German conditions: first, the formation of different confessional churches out of the Reformation, and, second, the building of states on a regional level, not on a national one as in other European countries. On this regional level, many independent states, called "territorial states," emerged during the fifteenth and sixteenth centuries, such as Saxony, Brandenburg, the Rhine Palatinate, and Bavaria–to name only the best known.

This presentation is organized into two main parts. First is an examination of confessionalism and state building as universal phenomena in early modern Europe, and second is an analysis of the German type of this general European development.[2]

[1]The phrase, "der deutsche Sonderweg," stands for the view that Germany failed to follow a western European (i.e., English or French) pattern of movement toward capitalism and a centralized state.

[2]In parts 1 and 2 through 4 respectively.

21

1

To study only the influences of Lutheranism on German state building during the sixteenth and seventeenth centuries is to mistake a part of a large problem for the whole. During the later Middle Ages and the ensuing Reformation era, there existed close connections all over Europe between religion and politics, which, though in theory bilateral, in fact gave the state and the princes the greatest advantages.

Laying aside the economic forces of the commercial revolution and early capitalism, which had a profound impact on both the Reformation and on politics, the European scene at the beginning of the early modern era was marked by two important changes. The first was the rise of the early modern state, as the medieval political institutions, which had been based chiefly on feudal (i.e., personal) bonds, took on the modern forms of bureaucratic administration, a distinct territory within marked boundaries, and a concentration of political power in a supreme, central institution, usually the person of a king or prince. The sovereign came to possess "sovereignty," as it was called in political thought since Jean Bodin's *Six Livres de la République* (1576). The second fundamental change was what I call "confessionalization," a religious change closely connected with the political one, just as in Latin Christendom the church and the state, religion and society, had always been closely interdependent, and would be until the French and Industrial Revolutions.[3]

"Confessionalization" is a far less familiar term than "state building," especially to British and American audiences, who are better acquainted with "denominations" as private religious associations than with state churches. The formation and development of "confessional churches" (*Konfessionkirchen*) are, by contrast, central topics in German history between the sixteenth and the nineteenth centuries. They were exclusively established, or at least privileged, creeds and ecclesiastical organizations within a particular society. The term "confessionalization" thus designates the fragmentation of the unitary Christendom (*Christianitas latina*) of the Middle Ages into at least three confessional churches—Lutheran, Calvinistic or "Reformed," and post-Tridentine Roman Catholic. Each formed a highly organized system, which tended to monopolize the world view with respect to the individual, the state, and society, and which laid down strictly formulated norms in politics and morals.

These confessional systems in both their civil and their ecclesiastical aspects are extremely visible in German history, because all three of them were

[3]In German usage, the term *Konfession* refers chiefly to the bodies of organized Christians who accept a certain interpretation of Christian doctrine. Thus, the Lutheran churches collectively belong to a single Lutheran confession. The term normally excluded the dissenting sects. The three chief confessions are thus Roman Catholic, Lutheran, and Reformed (here called "Calvinist"). The statement of doctrine on which such a community is based, called in English a "confession," is in German called a *Bekenntnis*.

represented within the Holy Roman Empire. In southern, western, and northern Europe, the significance of confessionalization was concealed by official religious homogeneity, Catholic in the cases of Spain and France, Lutheran in the Scandinavian kingdoms. Developments in seventeenth-century England, too, tended to obscure confessionalization, because the Puritan and Glorious Revolutions brought about an orderly and more or less peaceful coexistence between the Anglican state church and the private denominations, which lacked the status of confessional churches. Confessionalization was nonetheless important to early modern Europe as a whole. The grand process of state building between the fifteenth and the seventeenth centuries converged during the sixteenth and seventeenth centuries with confessionalization to transform the medieval *respublica christiana* into the early modern European landscape of independent powers and states. For at least one century, the link between state building and confessionalization was predominant in European history, that is, approximately from 1550 until 1650, in both foreign and domestic policy.

The impact of religious and confessional development on international relations is most evident for the first part of the Thirty Years' War (1618-48), though it goes back at least to the mid-sixteenth century, the age of the Netherlandish rebellion and war against Spain, which was a struggle between a Catholic power defending the Spanish empire on the one hand, and a Calvinist party of Dutch separatists on the other. Each side looked for allies among the other European powers, and, as the Czech historian Josef Polisensky[4] has shown, this search widened the political and confessional alliances into a Europe-wide phenomenon during the decades just before the Thirty Years' War. The struggle also became a conflict between two antagonistic social systems: the Protestant powers with republican attitudes and commercial interests, led by the Calvinistic Netherlands, and the Catholic monarchs and their court nobilities, led by Spain and Austria.

On the domestic side of state building, some early modern states already displayed typical features of the national state, though as yet indistinctly. In such states national bonds were weak, if they existed at all. Rather, it was religious, that is, *confessional*, uniformity that at the beginning of the early modern era supplied the basis for social integration. Modern sociologists might regard religion during the sixteenth and seventeenth centuries as the functional equivalent of national sentiment during the later eighteenth and nineteenth centuries. Religious and ecclesiastical institutions passed into the hands of the princes and their administrative staffs, helping them to replace medieval particularism with a unitary society of subjects. This is illustrated by the revocation of the Edict of Nantes in France in 1685 and by the ensuing persecution

[4]Josef Polisensky, *The Thirty Years War*, trans. Robert Evans (Berkeley-Los Angeles: University of California Press, 1971).

of the Huguenots in their semi-autonomous regions, some of which had been strongholds of political particularism and religious dissent since the Middle Ages. Whatever their individual positions, political thinkers of the sixteenth and seventeenth centuries emphasized in many variations the axiom, *religio vincula societatis*,[5] that is, law and order can only be sustained when all–or almost all–subjects of a state belong to the same religion or to the same church. Religion, they thought, was the best instrument to produce the voluntary obedience of subjects to princes and to establish harmony between the different estates and social classes.

2

The special German type of early modern development was characterized by sophisticated state building, which differed in two important respects from its counterpart in western and southwestern Europe. First, it was retarded by nearly half a century, and, secondly, it occurred not on a "national" level but on a regional and–in the case of the free cities–local level. The delay meant that the Reformation coincided with the critical stage of state building, and the small scale meant heavy competition between neighboring princes or between princes and town governments. The small sizes of states also meant face-to-face relations between rulers and subjects, giving the former opportunities for effective pressure on and effective control of the latter. Because of the Reformation and the subsequent formation of different theological, spiritual, and institutional aspects of church life, the German princes were able to increase their autonomy from the emperor and the Holy Roman Empire, as well as from their neighbors. Internally, through their assumption of the position of "guardians of the church" (*tutores ecclesiae*) and supreme heads of their respective territorial churches, the princes acquired the means from the churches to establish their sovereign power. Domestic sovereignty meant taming the political estates–the nobility as well as the larger towns–and integrating them into the state, now conceived in an absolutist sense.

Luther and Lutheranism by no means had a monopoly of this ecclesiastical support for princely state building on a territorial level. In Bavaria there existed a close alliance between the Catholic Counterreformation and the rise of the Wittelsbach state, which reached its climax under Duke (later Elector) Maximilian I. He worked together with the Jesuits at the University of Ingolstadt and at the new Jesuit secondary schools. The Jesuits became the tutors of the new political elite of ducal administrators and civil servants. It was the Jesuits, too, among them Maximilian's own confessor, Adam Contzen, who laid the theoretical and practical foundations of the early modern Bavarian state and who supported the dukes' aspirations to sovereignty (*Obrigkeit*). State intervention in ecclesiastical affairs was an essential

[5]Literally, "religion is the chain of society."

part of this change, which was approved by the popes, who recognized that the success of the Counter-Reformation in South Germany depended on the Wittelsbachs' strength and commitment.

The same alliance between church and territorial state existed in Calvinist regions, though with different theological arguments, institutions, and clergy. Detailed evidence has become available for the Rhine Palatinate, the leading Calvinist state during the sixteenth and early seventeenth centuries, and for the "Second Reformation," the shift from Lutheranism to Calvinism in various German territories around 1600, chief among them Brandenburg. Study of the county of Lippe in Westphalia proves that the Second Reformation was a crucial moment in state formation, especially in reducing the power of the territorial estates,[6] which had managed to take advantage of the first, Lutheran, Reformation. Their power was then checked by the second, Calvinist, Reformation. In Calvinist states, as in Lutheran ones, the Protestant churches received the status of official churches within territorial boundaries (*Landeskirchen*).[7] Such churches were dominated by the princes and their governments, even where Calvinist presbyteries were established as organs of ecclesiastical self-government, because the presbyteries were tied firmly to the hierarchy of territorial church and princely administration. The elders of the Calvinist churches in some states became a kind of bailiff who represented the early modern state on the local level.

3

The impact of confessionalization on the rise of the territorial state reveals three main aspects, which I shall treat in this order: first, the bureaucratic adminstration and its newly formed institutions; second, the widening field of state activity; and third, the position of the rulers, their dynasties, and their courts.

The bureaucracy experienced through the state building process a striking enlargement of personnel, as well as an expansion of the administration's competence, in the wake of both the Reformation and the Counter-Reformation. This is clearer in the Protestant territories, where—variations in names and institutional structure notwithstanding—we find everywhere a new and extensive structure of ecclesiastical administration. At the head were the consistories, composed of several consistorial councilors (*Konsistorialräte*) and presided over by a chairman (*Konsistorialpräsident*), who represented the ruler. Under them were superintendents or Lutheran bishops on the provincial level

---

[6]Territorial estates (*Landstände*), which existed in most major territories, were territorial parliaments composed of two to four houses of privileged groups of subjects (e.gg., nobles, towns, and clergy), who met periodically to deliberate on taxes, defense, and other issues.

[7]*Landeskirche* is the officially established (usually exclusive) church of a territorial state (*Land*).

and the village parsons. All were integrated into the new bureaucracy through recruitment by means of nomination, calling, and ordination, and through control by means of periodic visitations. They were all civil servants, bound to the system by a solemn oath taken on the respective church constitution (*Kirchenordnung*) and confession of faith.

The structure of ecclesiastical administration in Catholic states was more complex, though its sociopolitical functions and consequences were much the same as in Protestant states. In Bavaria, for example, a Spiritual Council (*Geistlicher Rat*) was established during the sixteenth century as the ecclesiastical department of the central administration. Half its members were civil servants and the other half clergymen nominated by the prince. Down to the end of the eighteenth century, this council remained the crucial instrument of Bavarian church policy, directing and controlling religious life rather as the consistories did in Lutheran and Calvinist territories.

The second impact of the Reformation was to widen the field of state activities. New branches of the territorial bureaucracy exercised manifold activities in areas formerly the domain of the medieval church, but which in the wake of the Reformation and Counter-Reformation were becoming domains of ever greater importance to the modern state. Among them were education and the schools, marriage and family life, welfare and poor relief, and nursing and midwifery. The fiscal system of the early modern state was also expanded through the direct or indirect control of ecclesiastical funds and properties by the state.

The Reformation's third area of impact on the state was the ruler's position. The alliance between confessional churches and the early modern state—still embodied in the person of the king or the prince—helped to put a certain distance between ruler and subject and to elevate the princes from the mass of ordinary persons, lay or clerical. As supporters of Luther and his Reformation, as promoters of the second, Calvinist, Reformation, or as preservers of the old Catholicism in its post-Tridentine dress, the rulers conquered the position of "first members of the church" (*praecipua membra ecclesiae*) or "defenders of the faith" (*defensores fidei*), that is to say, they became persons of paramount importance for their respective churches. Their decisions in religious and ecclesiastical affairs seemed of the greatest importance for the salvation of their subjects' souls. Though perhaps not approved by the theologians, in the eyes of ordinary subjects and churchgoers the princes and their families seemed to take a special position with regard to the deity. Furthermore, the impression made by the baroque courts as a kind of supernatural instance elevated the princes and their entourages and gave them a sacred aura. This was done through symbols and everyday rituals, such a the title "by the grace of God," which during the sixteenth century spread from the emperor and kings down to ordinary princes and even to town councilors. It also moved forward through prayers said in churches all over the territory on special occasions, such as a royal or princely accession, in wartime, at the signing of a treaty, and in everyday matters in the princely families, such as illness, pregnancy, or even merely a journey. Finally, the effect was achieved through days of thanksgiving and special services for a princely recovery from illness, the birth of a prince or princess, and on other occasions. Those who participated in such services must have carried away the impression of a direct relation between a dynasty's well-being and their own destinies.

The enlargement of the state's administrative institutions and activities, plus the sacralization of the ruler's person, strengthened the growing domestic sovereignty and made it more stable at a more decisive point in early modern state building. Coincidentally with its involvement in the Reformation and Counter-Reformation quarrels, the emerging sovereign state had to struggle fiercely against the traditional champions of the opposition to the centralized state, such as the privileged clergy, the nobility, and semi-autonomous towns. The sociologist Norbert Elias, in his well known *The Civilizing Process*,[8] describes early modern state building as a process of monopolizing of public functions by the state, as personified by the absolutist kings and princes. He argues that monopoly of military force and of taxation were the key monopolies in this process. Even if we accept Elias's analysis, we must still emphasize that in the German territorial state the monopoly of the church and religion, as enforced through the state's confessionalization, preceded and facilitated the monopolization of military force and taxation. The same applies to the cult of the ruler as practiced at the baroque courts, which has recently been described as a central element of seventeenth-century absolutism. This sacralization of the ruler would not have been possible without the rights over church affairs within its boundaries and over the religion of its subjects, which the state had conquered in the course of the Reformation and Counter-Reformation.

4

The alliance of territorial state building and confessionalization naturally influenced social relations and society as a whole, though we can study this impact only through the alliance of ecclesiastical and state interests on the local level. Here there developed the cooperation of pastor and bailiff, of pulpit and administration (*Kanzel und Amtshaus*), that engendered social control on the local level. This alliance guided the transformation of the dispersed, fragmentary medieval society of separate groups graded by privilege into the early modern society of the territorial state, a body of subjects, all uniformly equal before the state, well controlled and well regulated through the state's ever growing activity. Central government and the sovereign's

[8]Norbert Elias, *The Civilizing Process*, trans. Edmund Jephcott, 2 vols. (New York: Pantheon, 1977-1982).

will—at the beginning he was sovereign in theory only—took form in town and countryside in the persons of the local pastor and the local administrator. The parsons, whose activities reached down into the smallest villages and hamlets, were especially useful to the state in two ways. First, the state could use the pastors, who were closely connected to the ecclesiastical and civil hierarchies, both of which were controlled by the prince's central government, to spread its orders from the center down to its subjects in the most remote corners of the land. Second, the pastors could carry information in the contrary direction, supplying from the society's roots all the information the central government needed for realistic planning and for its ever expanding domestic activities, what contemporary parlance called "law and order" (*gute Policey*).

A sketch of how the church registers developed will illustrate the progress of the state building process. The registers are lists of births or baptisms, marriages, and deaths or burials in a given parish. Their beginning in Germany, roughly in the mid-sixteenth century, coincided with the rise of confessional churches. Kept by the pastors, when the ecclesiastical and civil bureaucracies were separated in the course of the nineteenth century, the registers remained in the churches' custody. During the early modern era, however they were both ecclesiastical and civil documents, affording the state and its bureaucracy their first authentic data on demographic development and the basic information needed for a population policy (*Peuplierungs-Politik*), so characteristic of the absolutist-mercantilist era of the seventeenth and eighteenth centuries.

Partly on the basis of the church registers which soon began to register illegitimate births separately, the state established a strict control of sexuality in favor of marriage, the enforcement of which served both to uphold Christian morality and to advance the state's population policy. Even in Protestant territories matrimonial matters remained *res mixtae*, subject to both spiritual and temporal jurisdiction, within the competence of the church. This meant that the state could regulate them only in alliance with the churches and through the appropriate ecclesiastical bodies, the ecclesiastical courts in Catholic and Lutheran lands, the presbyteries in Calvinist ones. Besides sexuality, many other everyday activities of individuals and social groups experienced sophisticated control and regulation through ecclesiastical institutions, all along lines directed by the state's interests. Elders and members of ecclesiastical courts had to exhort their communities' members to orderly conduct, cleanliness, diligence, and punctuality. They had to discourage drunkenness, swearing, and quarrelsomeness, and they were obliged to provide for a virtuous, orderly, and peaceful community. The family and household were special objects of their concern: they had to encourage servants and children to obedience and deference toward the heads of family and household; and fathers and mothers were admonished to fulfill their duties toward children and servants with respect to religious and secular education and to obedience and good conduct. Both material and spiritual needs of their dependents came within their purview, and public affairs were treated much as private ones were. Subjects were obliged to obedience toward the magistrates, the administrators, and especially the sovereign himself; administrators and magistrates were admonished to fulfill their duties correctly and zealously toward the state and the public.

Confessional church and confessional state combined to regulate religious and church life. They suppressed traditional forms of popular religion; they discouraged magical practices; and—more in Protestant than in Catholic lands—they tried to wipe out elements of popular medicine, rituals associated with the cycle of sowing and harvest, and popular amusements. Religious practices were standardized in accordance with norms laid down by the dominant church and the state. Though in some places special churches for dissenters or foreigners might be tolerated, they had to seek and gain permission for deviations in ritual from the established norms.

5

It is convenient to frame our conclusions under the rubric of "confessionalization," which suggests that the religious and ecclesiastical changes of the sixteenth and seventeenth centuries—what we roughly comprehend under the categories of "Reformation," "Second Reformation," and "Counter-Reformation"—were embedded in comprehensive social change. In Germany this process centered on the transformation of the old territorial dominion of the prince into a unitary state. It produced, on the one hand, the concentration of power in the ruler as possessor of sovereignty and, on the other, the institutional, territorial state of the early modern era. This state attempted to impose a rational way of life on its counterpart, the territorial society, which it understood as a uniform group of subjects. Though these subjects retained a hierarchy of prestige, rank, and honor—the keys to premodern social stratification in Europe—they lacked the old medieval distinctions in terms of inherited rights of lordship. The political and social effects of confessionalization worked in the same direction as other social forces, such as the advance of Roman law and Jean Bodin's new doctrine of sovereignty in the realm of jurisprudence.

An entire complex of forces thus combined in sixteenth and seventeenth-century Germany to produce the early modern state, with its institutionalized bureaucracy, its fixed boundaries, and its claims to sovereignty. The role of religious and ecclesiastical factors in this complex surely varied from state to state. We may say in general, however, that especially in the smaller and middling territories, besides the army and taxation—traditionally viewed as the decisive motives for centralization—the struggle for the control of a land's religious life and church structure, plus the control of the norms of belief, was of at least equal importance. The princely monopoly over the church was achieved earlier than monopolies over either the military forces or taxation, the two monopolies emphasized by Norbert Elias, whose perspective was based chiefly on western European history. The monopolization of the army and taxation, which was completed during the Thirty Years' War, was made much easier by the prior possession of an ecclesiastical monopoly, which also facilitated the adoption of the idea of sovereignty. Sovereignty characterized, according to Jean Bodin, the early modern concept of the state. Much the same may be said of the court as an instrument of monopolization in the service of the absolutist monarch, a point recently made in the spirit of Elias, for the "ritualization" of court life and the ruler's mode of life is unthinkable without the earlier integration of the church into the state.

The political effects of confessionalization were thus bound up with the concentration of political authority in the hands of a sovereign who stood above ordinary mortals, with the formation of a bureaucracy differentiated by function, and with the development of a unified, disciplined—perhaps we should say "tamed"—society. A comparison with other European states proves that these effects were by no means peculiar to Germany or to Lutheranism. Wherever the "German special path" began—if it began at all—Luther did not begin it, and Lutheran theology, at least in its sixteenth-century form, had no influence on its emergence. The peculiarities of German history originated in the simultaneity of political and ecclesiastical changes and in the small scale of territorial state building, and the German type of early modern development had its roots in a combination of Christian education—in its various confessional forms—as a means of social control with the sophisticated, intensive activities of the state. The latter was known in contemporary political thinking as "law and order" (*gute Policey*). This combination of confessional education and law and order produced results, the evaluation of which—good and bad—depends in part on individual opinions. For my own part, the education of civil servants to a special sense of duty toward and responsibility for the common good (*das gemeine Beste*) seems to me a positive achievement. It must be viewed dialectically, however, for its positive features engendered corresponding negative ones which dominated the longer run of German history. The more smoothly the state machine ran, and the more effective the administration became, the greater the gulf that grew between the ordinary subject and public affairs. In contrast to other European countries, such as the neighboring Netherlands or England, the concrete meaning of the ideal and the common good was not fixed in German lands in accordance with the wishes of the subjects and their representatives, but rather in a paternalistic or even autocratic manner by the rulers and their bureaucracies. The growing distance between subject and public affairs, together with the sacralization of the princes and their governments based on their functions as curators of religion (*tutores religionis*), became heavy burdens passed from the age of Reformation—and Counter-Reformation—to the German future.

Luther and the State: The Reformer's Teaching in Its Social Setting

Thomas A. Brady, Jr.
University of Oregon

IN THE HISTORY OF POLITICAL THOUGHT, Martin Luther's role is a small one. He took little part in one of the sixteenth century's chief intellectual creations: the emergence of the idea of the state as "an omnipotent yet impersonal power," as "a form of public power separate from both the ruler and the ruled, and constituting the supreme political authority within a certain defined territory."[1] The long prehistory of this idea reached from the recovery of Aristotle's *Politics* in the twelfth and thirteenth centuries via Scholastic doctors and Italian jurists and humanists to the Thomist revival in sixteenth-century Italy and Spain, until it bore fruit among the monarchomachs and politiques of Scotland, France, and England. The crucial step was the abandonment of the belief, held by Catholic tradition and Protestant reformers alike, that "one of the main aims of government must be to maintain 'true religion' and the Church of Christ." The Reformation's "paradoxical yet vital contribution" was to prove that rival confessions were willing to fight each other to the death, whereupon the politiques concluded that for the sake of civic peace "the powers of the State would have to be divorced from the duty to uphold any particular faith." The Wars of Religion thus completed what the Augustinian enemies of Thomas Aquinas—Luther included—had predicted and feared: the final victory of the Stagirite over the Galilean in the vindication of this world against the City of God.

Aristotle is by no means the only candidate for the role of intellectual progenitor of the European idea of the state. Another is Justinian's *Corpus iuris civilis*, advanced by Otto von Gierke in his thesis that the medieval recovery of Roman law undermined the Germanic sense of community. More broadly, classical literature in general and Cicero in particular have been named for this role by a series of writers ranging from Wilhelm Dilthey and Reinhold Niebuhr to Hans Baron, and J. G. A. Pocock who has argued most convincingly for the incompatibility of Augustinian Christianity with classical thought's rooting of politics in nature.[2] One day, perhaps, the candidacies will

---

[1] Quentin Skinner, *The Foundations of Modern Political Thought*, 2 vols. (Cambridge: Cambridge University Press, 1978), 2: 352, 358. The remaining quotes in this paragraph are from ibid., 352.

[2] J. G. A. Pocock, *The Machiavellian Moment: Florentine Political Thought and the Atlantic Republican Tradition* (Princeton: Princeton University Press, 1975), 552. See, in general, Wallace K. Ferguson, *The Renaissance in Historical Thought. Five Centuries of Interpretation* (Cambridge, Mass.: Houghton Mifflin, 1948), for older views.

merge, and the recoveries of Aristotle, Roman law, and classical literature will come to be seen as three parallel tunnels under the foundations of Latin Christianity's Augustinian vision. Martin Luther belongs not among the tunnelers but among the Augustinian rear-guard fighters against what Gibbon rightly saw as the ancient world's revenge on Christianity.

The idea of the state belongs to the age of Europe's transition from feudal to "modern" political organization, and it developed right along with the practice of statecraft and the assemblage of the state's arsenal—standing armies, bureaucracies, taxation, trade, and diplomacy.[3] We call the completed formation "the absolutist state" or "the early modern state," which emerged in the economically and socially advanced countries of Western Europe and was aped in the dependent societies of the East. The absolutist state was thus primarily a creation of the dominant core regions of capitalist agriculture, whence it was exported to the dominated semi-peripheral regions of the New Serfdom. Luther's homeland, Saxony, lay in the borderlands between these two zones of social development, which were to march—as Marx noted—along two different routes to capitalism and the modern age. Luther's Saxony was characterized by relatively advanced economic conditions and social relations—including a vigorous urban bourgeoisie heavily engaged in trade and mining, plus a fairly weak nobility—relatively weakly developed political particularism, and a strong princely authority resting on taxation, a civil bureaucracy, and wealth from the mines.

In what follows, Luther's teaching on government will be described and its proper social context identified. The conclusion will provide some reflections on why his teaching was later transformed into a doctrine of the state.

1

Luther's political intention cannot be doubted: he meant to strengthen government's authority. "If I had never taught or done anything else," he wrote in 1533,

> than that I had adorned and illuminated secular rule and authority, this alone should deserve thanks. . . . Since the time of the apostles, no doctor or writer, no theologian or lawyer, has confirmed, instructed, and comforted secular authority more gloriously and clearly than I was able to do through special divine grace.[4]

[3]Perry Anderson, *Lineages of the Absolutist State* (London: N. L. B., 1974), 29-37. A contrary view, which minimizes the significance of the absolutist state, is expressed by Dietrich Gerhard, *Old Europe: A Study of Continuity, 1000-1800* (New York: Academic Press, 1981), esp. 88-95.

[4]"Verantwortung der aufgelegten Aufruhr von Herzog Georg (1533)," in *WA* 38: 102, ll. 30 ff. (English: George W. Forell, *Faith Active in Love: An Investigation of the Principles Underlying Luther's Social Ethics* [Minneapolis: Augsburg, 1954], 122, n. 26). There is a nearly identical passage in "Ob Kriegsleute" (1526), in *WA* 19: 625, ll. 15-17 (English: *LW* 46: 95).

This "special divine grace" inspired the reformer to anchor his "adornment and illumination" of government in the submissive Pauline bedrock of Romans 13:1-7. He chose this voice from among the many in which the Bible spoke of temporal authority–Strasbourg's Martin Bucer, by contrast, chose the Book of Judges–and to his choice Luther's followers clung. All this is well known. Less familiar perhaps is Luther's effort to frame his political teaching in a comprehensive view of human society, much as his scholastic predecessors had done, though in Luther's case the attempt failed through his subordination of his political teaching to his theology.

As Luther during the 1510s found his way from Ockham through Augustine to Paul, he transformed the typically Augustinian antitheses–spirit-flesh, eternal-temporal, heavenly-earthly, future-present, hidden-open, invisible-visible, inward-outward, gospel-law–into a grand vision of reality cloven into two kingdoms,

> the temporal, which is ruled by the sword and is seen with the eyes, and the spiritual, ruled by grace and the forgiveness of sins.[5]

His discovery of justification by faith alone enabled Luther to relegate the Church in this world to the kingdom of this world (*regnum mundi*), which is also the kingdom of the Devil (*regnum diaboli*), where its claims to authority could be subjected to historical, philological, and functional criticism in the light of God's word. Luther's completed doctrine of the Two Kingdoms was thus Augustinian in origin but not in structure or spirit, for its different internal boundary line made possible–even necessary–his assault on the Church's claim to independent authority and social power in this world. This theology captivated the imaginations of many in his own day and vaulted the Saxon professor into a public career as a reformer of the Church.

Luther's doctrine of the Two Kingdoms became not the product but the starting point of his political teaching. During the winter of 1521-22, Luther returned from the Wartburg to Wittenberg, where his radicalized followers had taken control of his movement. Here, not during the Peasants' War of 1525, Luther first began to worry about social order. "But where is the order?" he asked the Wittenbergers in his Invocavit sermons during the week of March 9 through 16, 1522,

> for everything has been done recklessly without any order, to the scandal of the neighbors; whereas one ought first to have prayed on

[5]"Über das 1. Buch Mose, Predigten" (1523-4), in *WA* 24: 6, ll. 1-3. For orientation, see W. D. J. Cargill-Thompson, "The 'Two Kingdoms' and 'Two Regiments': Some Problems of Luther's *Zwei-Reiche-Lehre*," *Journal of Theological Studies*, n.s. 20 (1969): 164-85.

the matter and then consulted the authorities. Then one might be sure that the reforms came from God.[6]

Whether God's approval could be ascertained through the prayers or through the authorities' sanction, Luther did not say, but this sermon was the starting point of his political teaching.

Luther presented his political teaching first in *On Secular Authority* (1523), developed it through the Peasants' War pamphlets of 1525, and fixed it in *Whether Soldiers, Too, Can Be Saved* (1526). His teaching holds that this world's rulers are established by God to punish sins, keep the wicked in check, and help spread God's Word. The liberty and equality that reign in the invisible Church, over which Christ alone reigns, have no bearing on issues of law and order, justice and power, in this world. Resistance to authority is justified only if the ruler commands a violation of God's law, and then it may only be passive. Luther's commitment to authority was unswerving and unchangeable since the early 1520s. "I have always been," he wrote in 1525,

> and always will be on the side of those against whom insurrection is directed, no matter how unjust their cause. I am opposed to those who rise in insurrection, no matter how just their cause, because there can be no insurrection without hurting the innocent and shedding their blood.[7]

Luther tried during the 1520s to set this political teaching into a comprehensive doctrine of society. He chose the structure of Three Estates, which he adopted and adapted from Christian Aristotelianism and from the medieval catechetical tradition. The threefold division of society into clergy, warriors, and commons had arisen in the northern French heartland of feudalism around A.D. 1000., though it had undergone many changes during the following five centuries.[8] When Luther first employed the notion of Three

[6]"Invocavitpredigten" (1522), at March 9, 1522, in *WA* 10/III: 9, ll. 10-13. I cannot agree with Bernhard Lohse's opinion that these events brought not new developments but only greater precision in Luther's ideas. Bernhard Lohse, *Martin Luther. Eine Einführung in sein Leben und sein Werk* (Munich: Beck, 1981), 157-60. See also, for interpretations, Mark U. Edwards, Jr., *Luther and the False Brethren* (Stanford: Stanford University Press, 1975), 6-33; and Gert Haendler, *Luther on Ministerial Office and Congregational Function*, trans. Ruth C. Gritsch and Eric W. Gritsch, (Philadelphia: Fortress, 1981), 45-54.

[7]"Eine treue Vermahnung zu allen Christen" (1522), in *WA* 8: 690 (English: *LW* 45: 63).

[8]Georges Duby, *The Three Orders: Feudal Society Imagined*, trans. Arthur Goldhammer (Chicago: University of Chicago Press, 1980). The best analysis of Luther's teaching on the Three Estates is by Wilhelm Maurer, *Luthers Lehre von den drei Hierarchien un ihr mittelalterlicher Hintergrund*, Sitzungsberichte der Bayerischen Akademie der Wissenschaften, philosophisch-historische Klasse, 1970, no. 4 (Munich: Verlag der Bayerischen Akademie, 1970). The chief study in English of Luther's social thought is by F. Edward Cranz, *An Essay on the Development of Luther's*

Estates, before the Wittenberg disorders of the winter of 1521-22, he did so in the traditional way, presenting the estates as three different groups of persons. "God has established several estates," he wrote in 1519, "in which one is to test oneself and learn to suffer: for some the matrimonial, for others the ecclesiastical, and for yet others the political estate."[9] Gradually, however, he came to view the estates not as three social groups but as three networks or webs of social relations, to *each* of which *everyone* belongs. "First of all," he wrote in later years,

> you must be a part of a family, a father or mother, a child, servant, or maid. Second, you must live in a city or in the country as a citizen, a subject, or a ruler. Third, you are part of the Church, perhaps a pastor, an assistant, a sexton, or in some other way a servant of the Church, if only you have and hear the Word of God.[10]

These are the three estates founded by God, as he wrote in 1528:

> But the holy orders and true institutes founded by God are these three: the priestly office, the matrimonial estates, the temporal authority. . . . Therefore, such three institutes or orders are encompassed by God's Word and ordinances.[11]

The importance of this change—from estates as social groups to estates as modes of social relationships—lies in the fact that Luther's estates no longer serve as discrete loci of various rights and modes of authority, so that there is no social basis for divided or decentralized authority, and hence no basis for opposition to temporal authority. The social relations are rooted not in nature or human custom but in God's ordinance for this world.

Luther's famous doctrine of "calling" (*vocatio, Beruf*) is part of his larger doctrine of the Three Estates, a point sufficiently understood by none of the participants in the famous debate sparked by Max Weber.[12] The allegedly revolutionary aspect of his doctrine of calling—the attribution of ethical worth

Thought on Justice, Law, and Society, Harvard Theological Studies 19 (Cambridge, Mass.: Harvard University Press, 1959). His interpretation of the Three Estates is marred by a misconception about the tradition, which leads him to exaggerate the innovative character of Luther's ideas—a common enough mistake among Luther scholars.

[9]"Ein Sermon von dem Sakrament der Taufe" (1519), in *WA* 2: 734, ll. 20-28.

[10]*WA TR* 6: 266, ll. 16-27, no. 6913 (English: Forell, *Faith*, 123).

[11]"Vom Abendmahl Christi. Bekenntnis (1528)," in *WA* p. 26: 504, ll. 31; p. 505, l. 10.

[12]The basic work is Gustaf Wingren, *Luther on Vocation* (Philadelphia: Fortress, 1957), translated from the Swedish, but the present state of the question is best described by Werner Conze, "Beruf," in *Geschichtliche Grundbegriffe. Historisches Lexikon zur politisch-sozialen Sprache in Deutschland* I (Stuttgart: E. Klett, 1972): 390-407, here at 402.

to secular trades and occupations—in fact capped a long evolution which began, like so much else that came to fruition in Luther's time, in the twelfth century. Most commentators have construed Luther's teaching much too individualistically, viewing the calling as a personal attribute, whereas Luther taught that in this world (*coram mundo*) one never stands alone but always in social relationships, for each is "bound in this life to another person."[13] Callings are therefore also social relationships, and they form the internal structures of the Three Estates.

By the end of the 1520s Luther's doctrine of Three Estates had evolved completely along two main lines. First, he established the principle of centralized hierarchy within the estates and related them analogically to one another. Second, he struggled to coordinate this teaching with the Church's unique participation in both kingdoms. Luther's principle of centralized hierarchy, to turn to the first point, is not feudal but patriarchal, derived by analogy through the partriarchal household from God's patriarchal management of creation. The social analogy between the household—Luther's "matrimonial estates"—and government is expressed most forcefully, and perhaps most effectively, in the *Larger Catechism* of 1529 under the rubric of the Fourth Commandment. "For all the other forms of authority," he wrote,

> flow from and are extensions of parental authority. ... . Thus all those who are called "lords" stand in the parents' stead and necessarily take their power and authority from [the parental office]. Therefore the Bible calls them all "fathers," because they exercise in their rule the office of a father and ought to regard their folk with a fatherly heart. Just as, many years ago, the Romans and others called the lords and ladies of the household ... "fathers and mothers of the household," so they called their princes and rulers ... "fathers of their country."[14]

The ruler is father of his land, according to Luther, the father is ruler of his household, and the authority of each derives from and reflects God's authority over the world. Political and domestic rulers are bulwarks against sin and against the Devil, who seeks to make this world his kingdom (*regnum diaboli*). Although political rule is derived from domestic rule, the father has no authority against the prince, though neither does the prince's authority invade the household. Luther thus stopped several steps short of true absolutism and the practical realization of the maxim "princeps legibus solutus," according to which all subjects stand as naked individuals before the ruler's will. The analogy with Luther's view of the individual before God is tempting, though we

---

[13]"Auslegung der Bergpredigt (1530-32)," in *WA* 32: 390, ll. 33-34.

[14]"Deudsch [Grosser] Catechismus (1529)," in *WA* 19: 152, ll. 20-35.

must not allow apparent logic and symmetry to distort our view of his teaching. He was at most a forerunner of absolutism, and his teaching on the domestic and political estates is clear and roughly symmetrical.

The same cannot be said of his teaching on the third estate, the Church.[15] Luther could not, and did not, make the Church into a distinct, hierarchically organized and centralized order of this world, analogous to the other two estates, because his doctrine of the Church had already taken fixed form from his theology. On the one hand, the form of the true, invisible Church (*ecclesia invisibilis*) in the Kingdom of God was that of an egalitarian priesthood of believers, ruled by Christ alone. In his vindication of this conception, Luther had denied the Church in this world any independent authority at all. On the other hand, Luther could never bring himself to identify the egalitarian, true Church as a model for the visible Church (*ecclesia visibilis*) in the form of a congregation of equals. There is evidence that he did think in this direction during the early 1520s, when he emphasized the priesthood (*sacredotium*) in a congregational sense, but by 1523 he began to veer toward an idea of the Church as a structure of offices (*ministerium*).[16] The timing of the shift fits the evolution of his thought on government and on the Three Estates.

For Luther the Church was thus one of the Three Estates, except that, unlike the other two, it had no internal principle of centralized, hierarchical authority. This is so because Luther's ecclesiology lay precisely at the line of juncture between his theology and his social teaching, between the Two Kingdoms and the Three Estates. Here his theology truly shaped his social thought, for his theologically grounded denial of autonomous authority to the Church interfered with every German Protestant attempt to reconstitute genuinely clerical power—what its lay critics called "a new papacy."[17] The consequent asymmetry, however, in the Three Estates left the relationship between Church and government "disputed and indeterminate."[18] The priesthood of believers retained just enough power to block justifications for reconstruction of clerical power, though not enough to shape the Church in the world.

[15]There is no comprehensive study in English of Luther's ecclesiology. For a clear, judicious presentation, see Jaroslav Pelikan, *The Christian Tradition. A History of the Development of Doctrine*, vol. 4: *Reformation of Church and Dogma (1300-1700)* (Chicago: University of Chicago Press, 1984), 172-75. For more detail, see Haendler, *Luther on Ministerial Office*, and for a sober judgment from a neutral perspective, see Sheldon S. Wolin, "Luther: The Theological and the Political," in his *Politics and Vision: Continuity and Innovation in Western Political Thought* (Boston: Little, Brown, 1960), 141-61.

[16]On the state of this question, see Haendler, *Luther on Ministerial Office*, 17-20.

[17]Steven Ozment, *The Reformation in the Cities: The Appeal of Protestantism to Sixteenth-Century Germany and Switzerland* (New Haven: Yale University Press, 1975), 151-66.

[18]The phrase is Wilhelm Maurer's in *Luthers Lehre*, 124. Lohse, *Martin Luther*, 187, summarizes the state of the question and notes the lack of program in Luther's teaching.

The anomalous character of the Church, which was caused by theoretical disconformity of Luther's Three Estates to his Two Kingdoms, lay behind all those queer arrangements in the Lutheran territorial churches, such as consistorial presidents and superintendent, the prince as "emergency bishop" (*Notbischof*) and "first member of the church" (*praecipuum membrum ecclesiae*), and the princely *cura religionis* and *jus in sacra*.[19] Many such creative improvisations endured until the November Revolution and the Weimar Constitution swept them all away.

2

What kind of social background does Luther's teaching suggest? The answer must be: a society no longer feudal but not yet absolutist. The vehemence of his teaching also indicates a frantic concern for order, which may in turn reflect his experience in a society in great flux. Both conditions fit Luther's Saxony.[20] The land lacked both a strongly privileged, corporately organized nobility and a communally organized peasantry, and its lively, booming cities lacked the strongly corporate traditions of the South German towns. In the towns and the mining districts, however, there was great mobility of persons and capital. Luther's own social background—his father's peasant roots and financial successes, his mother's roots in town, and his own lack of a true home town—illustrates these conditions in the transition zone between the older, more rooted societies of western and southern Germany and the classic colonial lands of the German East.

Luther grew up in a relatively fluid society, a Saxony poised between its colonial past and its future plunge into the "New Serfdom" and absolutism. The one sturdy force for law and order in this land was the territorial prince and his bureaucracy,[21] and in Luther's Saxony the prince's power and stature were swollen by the rivers of silver and copper that poured from the mines and smelters into his coffers. Saxony lacked the communal federations which furnished alternative forces for law and order in southern Germany, and he thus had no experience with ordinary folk taking law and order into their own capable hands.

---

[19]Lewis W. Spitz, "Luther's Ecclesiology and his Concept of the Prince as 'Notbischof,'" *Church History* 22 (1953): 113 ff.; Johannes Heckel, *Cura religionis, ius in sacra, ius circa sacra*, 2d ed. (Darmstadt: Wissenschaftliche Buchgesellschaft, 1962).

[20]See Karlheinz Blaschke, *Sachsen im Zeitalter der Reformation*, Schriften des Vereins für Reformationsgeschichte, no. 185 (Gütersloh: Gerd Mohn, 1970), plus his contribution to this volume; and Adolfe Laube, *Studien über den erzgebirgischen Silberbergbau von 1470 bis 1546*, 2d ed., Forschungen zur mittelalterlichen Geschichte, 22 (Berlin: Akademie Verlag, 1976).

[21]See Ingetraut Ludolphy, *Friedrich der Weise, Kurfürst von Sachsen 1463-1525* (Gottingen, 1984), 239-52, 281-366; and see Karlheinz Blaschke's contribution to this volume.

Such conditions help to explain why Luther so mistrusted the common people of his day. This world, he wrote, "cannot endure where there is no inequality of persons, so that some are free and some bound, some are lords and some subjects."[22] Though patently false if applied to South German and Swiss conditions, the statement perhaps reflected reality in Luther's Saxony, which lacked the social basis for political institutions based on communalism. It is worth noting that the most radical programs of 1525–from Thomas Müntzer's communism of the just, to Hans Herrgott's revolutionary communism, to Luther's thoroughgoing authoritarianism–arose in the Franconian-Thuringian borderlands between southern and eastern Germany.[23] The peoples of these lands lived close enough to the South to be aware of the dense networks of corporate institutions there, but they mostly lacked the everyday experience of ordinary folk settling their own affairs. Luther himself knew that in a few far corners of the Holy Roman Empire–he mentioned Switzerland and Ditmarsh–"many of the Common Man" ruled themselves,[24] but to him authority (*Obrigkeit*) always meant a king, prince, or other nobleman.

It has often been alleged that Luther condemned popular insurrection only after the rebels in 1525 claimed religious authority for their actions. This is false. Luther believed deeply in both social inequality and submission to authority as the only possible foundations of social order. Where this order is disrupted, he once wrote,

> the mob [*der Pöfel*] is the Devil. God performs through it what he would otherwise do through the Devil to punish the wicked. Thus the people become rebellious when God removes from their hearts fear of and regard for authority.[25]

The Revolution of 1525 and the specter of Thomas Müntzer, its prophet and Luther's former disciple, fixed forever in Luther's heart the fear of self-help by the Common Man. "For what God wants," he preached in 1528,

---

[22]"Ermahnungen zum Frieden" (1525), in *WA* 18: 327, ll. 6-8. I discuss this theme in greater detail in "Luther's Social Teaching and the Social Order of His Age," in Gerhard Dunnhaupt, ed., *The Martin Luther Quincentennial* (Detroit: Wayne State University Press, 1985), 270-90; and more briefly in my "Two Kingdoms or Three Estates? Tradition and Experience in Luther's Social Teaching," in *Lutherjahrbuch* 52 (1985) (=*Martin Luther 1483-1983. Werk und Wirkung / Work and Impact. Referate und Berichte des Sechsten Internationalen Kongresss für Lutherforschung, Erfurt, DDR, 14.-20. August 1983*, ed. Helmar Junghans [Göttingen: Vandenhoeck & Ruprecht, 1985]): 197-212.

[23]The programs are discussed by Peter Blickle, *The Revolution of 1525: The German Peasants' War from a New Perspective*, trans. Thomas A. Brady, Jr., and H. C. Erik Midelfort (Baltimore: Johns Hopkins University Press, 1981), 145-54.

[24]*WA TR* 4: 240, ll. 43-44, no. 4342 (1539), and see "Ob Kriesleute (1526)," in *WA* 19: 635, ll. 17-18.

[25]*WA TR* 2: 314, no. 2982.

that He sufficiently ordains and commands. God does not sleep, He is no fool, and He knows quite well how to govern. Therefore, it is not your task, leave it be, and do not pick up the sword.

Against this it commonly happens that someone says: 'There is no good government and much violence and injustice. We must do something about it.' When the mob [*der Pöbel*] hears such words, it takes them up and responds: 'So, let's do it.' For the old Adam is so great a fool that he neglects and omits what is commanded, and he undertakes what is not commanded. What moved Müntzer, if not the notion that government is bad, so we must make it Christian?

This is the bellows that puffs up and inflames the people's hearts. Thus, when the cry goes out, 'Justice! Justice! Injustice! Injustice!' no one says to himself: 'Is that my job?' You aren't the one who ought to establish justice and punish injustice. When some wrong is done in my house, and my next door neighbor wants to break into my house and do justice there, what should I say to that?[26]

Luther had never depended on his fellows either for justice or for his livelihood, and it was not his fellows but his princes who protected and saved him and his reformation. It was a lesson he never forgot.

Luther's deep fear of disorder and mistrust of the Common Man endured through his later career. They were not touched by his volte-face after the Diet of Augsburg in 1530, when he reversed his condemnation of resistance to the emperor. At most this decision, which smoothed his prince's path into the Schmalkaldic League, represents a shift in his location of true authority (*Obrigkeit*) from the emperor to the princes. Nor did the famous affirmation of resistance by Lutheran pastors at Magdeburg in 1550 contradict this picture, for the principle involved there—the duty of inferior magistrates to resist under certain circumstances—derived from Martin Bucer and Landgrave Philip of Hesse, not from Luther and Saxony.[27] The right to resistance was endorsed with enthusiasm nowhere in Lutheran Germany. Finally, Heinz Schilling's discovery that under certain circumstances, as in the city of Lemgo against the count of Lippe, Lutheranism could strengthen the defense of corporate rights against a centralizing prince, hardly disturbs the general picture.[28]

[26]"Wochenpredigten über Johannis 16-20," at December 5, 1528, in *WA* 28: p. 246, ll. 35-36, and p. 247, ll. 1-10.

[27]Skinner, *Foundations* (as note 1), 2: 204-6.

[28]Because the resistance does not sem to have been connected with any specifically Lutheran doctrine. See Heinz Schilling's contribution to this volume; and for another example of close alliance between the corporate power of a citizenry and Lutheranism, see Joachim Whaley, *Religious Toleration and Social Change in Hamburg, 1529-1819*, Cambridge Studies in Early Modern History (Cambridge: Cambridge University Press, 1985), 13-22.

In summary, Luther's mature theology, especially his doctrine of the Two Kingdoms, blocked the path to a coherent, symmetrical conception of social order in the form of the doctrine of Three Estates. This blockage is particularly visible in the anomalous status and structure of the Church in Luther's teaching. Although the domestic and political estates are linked through a social analogy of paternal and political authority, Luther's doctrine of authority has little kinship with western European ideas of the state. At most his teaching may be assigned to the category of proto-absolutist notions of authority, and it is worth noting that his biblical justification, the Pauline injunctions in Romans 13:1-7, was later taken up by apologists for absolutism, including the French Catholic bishop Jacques-Bénigne Bossuet.[29] Luther certainly aided such developments through his weakening of the state's chief rival, the Church, and his denial of religious meaning to oppositional, corporate institutions, but he was hardly a major spokesman for absolutism. He never even reached the point of separating the principle of authority from the person of the ruler.

3

If Luther's political teaching was old-fashioned even in his own day, how did he come in recent times to be regarded as a major progenitor of the idea of the authoritarian state? He certainly did not enjoy any such reputation at the time of the French Revolution. Note the following prayer:

> O Jesus and Luther, holy patron saints of freedom, who in your hours of humiliation seized and with gigantic strength broke humanity's chains, look down now from your heights upon your descendants, and rejoice for the crops that sprang from the seeds you sowed and are now waving in the wind.[30]

The year was 1793, when the Committee of Public Safety ruled in Paris, and the suppliant was Johann Gottlieb Fichte, philosopher of the Prussian state. His colleague, the Swabian Hegel, once wrote that "political liberty and the public rule of law are purely the fruit of the rediscovered freedom in God."

The myth of Luther as prophet of the state belongs among the legends of 1871, and it was created by those Protestant intellectuals, such as Heinrich von Treitschke and Albrecht Ritschl, who hoped to meld Protestant Christianity

---

[29]Skinner, *Foundations* (as note 1), 2: 113.

[30]This and the following quotation are taken from Heinrich Bornkamm, *Luther im Spiegel der deutschen Geitsesgeschichte,* 2d ed. (Göttingen: Vandenhoeck & Ruprecht, 1970), 220-21, 237.

with the new Germany's power into a German Christian civilization.[31] Their respective addresses on Luther's 400th birthday in 1883 are shot through with this vision. Treitschke, speaking at Darmstadt, hoped that Luther would one day soon be recognized as the teacher of all Germans, while Ritschl told his audience at Göttingen that the Reformation's chief social benefits were to strengthen the rulers and to immunize their subjects against the virus of revolution. Such men formulated the essence of the Luther-to-Bismarck thesis, which became a direct forerunner of the twentieth century's Luther-to-Hitler thesis. It held that 1871 brought the culmination of what had begun in 1517. Gradually Luther was outfitted with a full-blown doctrine of the state, which held that the state enjoyed autonomy (*Eigengesetzlichkeit*) from the principles of natural and Christian morality.

The myth of Luther's doctrine of the state was useful in two ways. First, it removed the problem of Christian morality from politics and kept it from complicating Germany's grasp for world power in competition with the predatory empires of Britain and France. In this German Protestantism was more honest than much of its British counterpart, which simply identified Christianity with British morality, culture, and interests. Second, Luther's alleged doctrine enhanced the state's authority in the form of the German monarchy. It did so not because of authoritarianism as an abstract ethical value, but because any devolution of political power in Imperial Germany strengthened, or would strengthen, Protestantism's foes. Chief among these were a politically awakened Catholicism, called "ultramontanism" by the Protestants, and a vigorous Social Democracy. German Protestantism during the generation before 1914 lay properly skewered on the horns of a terrible dilemma: industrialization, which made the new Germany strong, also delivered the Protestant masses into the hands of atheistic Socialism. Thus the very forces that gave Germany a chance at world power would assure that this world power would not be a solidly Protestant Christian power. The patterns of industrialization, urbanization, and elections in Wilhelmine Germany all confirm Social Democracy's theft of the masses from their old Protestant churches. Hence the importance of Luther as a teacher not of an abstract doctrine of obedience to the state, but of obedience to the German monarchy had been produced by history. This is the meaning of the saying that the Prussian state rested on three foundations: throne, bayonet, and catechism.

---

[31]Heinrich von Treitschke, "Luther and the German Nation," in his *Germany, France, Russia, and Islam* (New York, 1915), esp. 259-60; Albrecht Ritschl, "Festival Address (Göttingen, November 10, 1883)," trans. David W. Lotz, *Ritschl and Luther: A Fresh Perspective on Albrecht Ritschl's Theology in Light of his Luther Study* (Nashville: Abingdon, 1974), esp. 189-90. This entire line of interpretation is summed up by Heinrich Boehmer's *Luther in the Light of Recent Research*, trans. C. F. Huth, Jr. (New York: The Christian Herald, 1916), esp. 318, for the view that Luther destroyed one civilization and created another.

If the Wilhelmine Luther had been a monarchist, under the Weimar Republic he became a counterrevolutionary. With the state now in the hands of Protestantism's political enemies, the Weimar Coalition of Catholics and Socialists, the Luther of the 1920s became a figure of opposition, just as he appears in Gerhard Ritter's Christian-nationalist biography, published in 1925.[32] It was theologians, however, the proponents of the "Luther renaissance," who wielded Luther as a weapon in the service of national counter-revolution.[33] Such scholars as Paul Althaus, Emanuel Hirsch, and later Heinrich Bornkamm, whom Klaus Scholder has dubbed the "folkish theologians," spoke for an alliance between the Christian-nationalist and the racial-nationalist oppostions to the republic, and greeted Hitler's coming to power as, in Althaus's words, "the German hour of the Church."[34] They, before all others, are responsible for lending false credence to the notion that Luther was a forerunner of Adolf Hitler.

Luther's role as prophet of the authoritarian state, though it was prepared before World War I, was really a product of the 1930s. We find it in Nazi propaganda, in W. H. Auden's poem, "September 1, 1939,' and in Thomas Mann's wartime essays and speeches. This Luther is not a creation of the Protestant Reformation but a devising of Protestant theologians and publicists between 1871 and 1933.

Luther's political teaching was neither very coherent nor, it seems, very profound. It was too much shaped by his theology, by the strategies and opportunities of Reformation politics, and by his own, limited social perceptions, to have much general validity. It certainly does not rank among the major efforts to interpret the new kind of government, the early modern state, that was emerging in his age, such as those of Machiavelli and Bellarmine, Vitoria and Molina, Seyssel and Hotman, or Buchanan and Hobbes. Luther's teaching is important historically because of his followers' use of it to support the link between churches and princes the German Reformation had produced. To link his authentic teaching, however, with Europe's catastrophes during the past seventy years is to swallow the illusions that lay behind both the wishful thinking of Treitschke and Ritschl and the apocalyptic desperation of the folkish theologians.

[32]Gerhard Ritter, *Luther–Gestalt und Symbol* (Munich: F. Bruckman, 1925). The English version, *Luther: His Life and Work*, trans. John Riches (New York: Harper & Row, 1963), is based on a much-revised later edition.

[33]Karl Kupisch, "The 'Luther Renaissance,'" *Journal of Contemporary History* 2, (October 1967): 39-49.

[34]I refer to Klaus Scholder, *Die Kirchen und das Dritte Reich*, vol. 1: *Vorgeschichte und Zeit der Illusionen 1918-1934* (Frankfurt/M: Ullstein, 1977), 125-30. For this stream of thought, see James A. Zabel, *Nazism and the Pators: A Study of the Ideas of Three Deutsche Christen Groups*, American Academy of Religion, Dissertation Series, No. 14. (Missoula, Mont.: Scholars Press, 1976), 51-109.

We haven't to seek far to find the motive for perpetuating the Luther-to-Hitler legend. As a general rule, those who want to blame the past also want to exculpate the present, or at least to justify some present policy or action which could otherwise not stand scrutiny. The Luther-to-Hitler legend has had just such a purpose, for it was created to mobilize Luther's prestige and the authority of history in general for a vision which contradicted all recent experience. Small wonder that other Europeans quickly adopted what German chauvinists had created. Together they have continued to spread one of the great modern lies: that the catastrophic wars of our century are the inevitable consequences of the deep past, rather than the suicide of Europe's bourgeois civilization.

Luther and the State:
Post-Reformation Ramifications

Eric W. Gritsch
Lutheran Theological Seminary
Gettysburg, Pennsylvania

IN LUTHER RESEARCH, MUCH DEPENDS ON THE APPROACH to the evidence, just as mountain climbers depend on the correct approach to a mountain, the *Einstieg*, to reach the peak. Since Luther developed his ideas in response to specific questions and events, the massive collection of Lutherania suffers from Luther's unsystematic arrangement. Moreover, all sorts of hermeneutical questions have been imposed on Luther—for reasons ranging from the fury of systematic theologians in search of the a-historical Luther to the pedantry of historians in quest for the historical Luther.

The debate between Karl Holl and Ernst Troeltsch is a case in point. Holl's defense of Luther as the pioneer of the modern culture state (*Kulturstaat*)[1] was strongly challenged by Ernst Troeltsch, who was influenced by the sociologist Max Weber and therefore produced a massive revisionist history of "the social teaching of the Christian churches."[2] Troeltsch concluded that Luther and mainline Protestants are defenders of medieval Christendom rather than pioneering advocates of modern culture, and he singled out Luther's idea of the state to prove his point. According to Troeltsch, Luther's views were naive as well as contradictory: on the one hand, Luther had demanded that the state be freed from subordination to medieval ecclesiastical hierarchy; on the other hand, he had viewed the state as an entity divinely ordained to protect the world against the massive onslaught of evil which is manifested in disorder and lawlessness. Because rulers had become more and more absolutist since the sixteenth century, especially in Germany, Troeltsch concluded that Luther had merely pioneered a transition from divinely instituted state authority to territorial absolutism. He contended that this absolutism was paticularly visible in Prussian Lutheranism, which applied the phrase "by the grace of God" to both king and local authorities.[3]

---

[1] *The Cultural Significance of the Reformation*, tr. Karl and Barbara Hertz and John Lichtblau (New York: Meridian, 1959), 53. The German text is in Volume 1 of *Gesammelte Aufsätze zur Kirchengeschichte: Luther*, 4th and 5th eds. (Tübingen: Mohr, 1927), 468-543.

[2] *The Social Teachings of the Christian Churches*, 2 vols., tr. Oliver Wyon (New York: Macmillan, 1931). German edition 1922.

[3] Ernst Troeltsch, *Protestantism and Progress: A Historical Study of the Relation of Protestantism to the Modern World*, tr. W. Montgomery (New York: Putman's Sons, 1912), 111-13.

Troeltsch contended that the modern state, with its laws regarding individual freedom and democracy, is rooted not in Luther and the mainline Reformation movement (labeled "Church Protestantism") but instead in the radical Protestantism of Anabaptists, Spiritualists, and Puritans (labeled "Sectarianism"). But Sectarian affirmations of religious liberty and freedom of conscience won the day only under the influence of the eighteenth-century Enlightenment, which "secularized" them by grounding them in Graeco-Roman philosophical notions of human nature and political life. When they became linked with "the democratic awakening of the masses" and with the "Romantic idea of the National Spirit," they served as the philosophical foundation for the modern state, particularly in America.[4] According to Troeltsch, Luther could not be the pioneer of Holl's modern *Kulturstaat* because he proposed an unrealistic balance between the Christian gospel and civil law. Luther had first expected Christians to obey civil laws voluntarily out of love for their neighbor. But when he discovered that most Christians failed to live that way, he tried to combine Christian sacrificial love with the idea of "natural law"; though Christians are inwardly governed by love, they are outwardly bound to obey civil authorities. The result was a "super-idealistic, almost Utopian" view of the state, which prompted German Lutherans to separate private from public morality.[5] Some of Troeltsch's disciples, among them Reinhold Niebuhr, viewed such a moral stance as the seedbed for tyranny, and they accused Luther of being the spiritual father of Adolf Hitler since Hitler appealed to a Lutheran ethos when he demanded absolute loyalty to the state.[6]

In light of such judgments, it is quite obvious that Luther's views have generated historiographical problems with regard to the influence of the Middle Ages on the genesis of his thought (*Entstehungsgeschichte*) and to their historical impact (*Wirkungsgeschichte*). This article deals with the latter. First, the basic features of Luther's view of the state, which are rooted in his theological reflections, will be presented; next, a sketch of the history of the propagation of his views; and finally, some reflections on the validity of his view in our time.

---

[4]Ibid., 117-27. Troeltsch viewed Puritanism as "a sublimated essence of the 'Free Church,'" Anabaptist, Spiritualist-subjectivist ideas in combination with the old Calvinistic idea of the inviolability of Divine Majesty" (121). This interpretation of Puritanism is debatable in the light of later research in the left wing or Radical Reformation. Although continental radical reformers had contacts with English Puritans (in the Netherlands), their historical roots and religious ideas separated rather than united them. See George H. Williams, *The Radical Reformation* (Philadelphia: Westminster Press, 1962), 865.

[5]Troeltsch, *The Social Teaching of the Christian Church*, 508, 547-54.

[6]Reinhold Niebuhr, *The Nature and Destiny of Man*, 2 vols. (New York: Charles Scribner's Sons, 1953), 2, 194-95. This view has been made popular in England after World War II and in the United States by William L. Shirer, *The Rise and Fall of the Third Reich* (New York: Charles Scribner's Sons,1959), 236. See the critical analysis of this view by Peter C. Matheson, "Luther and Hitler: A Controversy Reviewed," *Journal of Ecumenical Studies* 17 (1980): 445-53.

Luther's View of the State

Luther research has not produced any consensus on the so-called Two Kingdoms doctrine, a designation Luther himself did not use.[7] Luther, of course, was a biblical theologian and developed his views in a specific historical context wherein he judged the church, rather than the state, to be the source of tyranny. "It seems plain to me," Luther told his students during his lecture on Romans 13:1 ("Let every person be subject to the governing authorities")

> that in our day the secular powers are carrying on their duties more successfully and better than the ecclesiastical rulers are doing. For they are strict in their punishment of thefts and murders, except to the extent that they are corrupted in insidious privileges. But the ecclesiastical rulers, except for those who invade the liberties, privileges, and rights of the church, whom they condemn to excessive punishments, actually nourish pride, ambitions, prodigality, and contentions rather than punish them (so much so that perhaps it would be safer if the temporal affairs of the clergy were placed under secular power).[8]

This judgment reflected the good relationship Luther enjoyed with the rulers of Electoral Saxony: Frederick the Wise (1486-1525) who never met with Luther, using the court chaplain George Spalatin as go-between; Frederick's brother John (1525-32) who was committed to Luther's reform movement; and John's son, John Frederick (1532-47) who regarded Luther as his spiritual father.[9]

---

[7]The term "two kingdoms doctrine" (*Zwei-Reiche-Lehre*) was first used by Harald Diem, *Luthers Lehre von den zwei Reichen*, 1938. Reprinted in Gerhard Sauter, ed. *Zur Zwei-Reiche-Lehre Luthers*, Theologische Bücherei, Neudrucke und Berichte aus dem 20. Jahrhundert, vol. 49 (Munich: Kaiser,1973), 3-175. See also Sauter's essay on the problem, ibid., vii-xiv, and the bibliographical essay by Johannes Haun, ibid., 217-45. The hermeneutical function of Luther's view of the two kingdoms has been explored by Martin Honecker, "Die Weltverantwortung des Glaubens. Zur ethisch-politisch Dimension der Theologie Luthers," in *Luthers Sendung für Katholiken und Protestanten*, ed. Karl Lehmann (Freiburg: Schnell and Steiner, 1982). A balanced summary treatment is offered by Heinrich Bornkamm, *Luther's Doctrine of the Two Kingdoms*, tr. Karl H. Hertz (Philadelphia: Fortress Press, 1966). Luther did not develop a full-fledged doctrine of two realms, but "consoled consciences in certain situations" (*situationsbezogener Gewissenszuspruch*). See Hans-Joachim Gänssler, *Evangelium und weltliches Recht. Hintergrund, Entstehungsgeschichte and Anlass von Luthers Scheidung zweier Reiche oder Regimente*, Veröffentlichungen des Instituts für europäische Geschichte Mainz, Abteilung für abendländische Religionsgeschichte 109 (Wiesbaden: Steiner, 1983), 155.

[8]"Lectures on Romans, 1515-16," *D. Martin Luthers Werke, Kritische Gesamtausgabe* (Weimar: Böhlau, 1883-), 56: 478.26-32. Hereafter cited *WA*. *Luther's Works* (American Edition), ed. Jaroslav Pelikan and Helmut Lehmann (Philadelphia: Fortress Press and St. Louis: Concordia Press, 1955-), 25: 471. Hereafter cited *LW*.

[9]For a detailed analysis of Luther as political advisor to the three Electors see Hermann Kunst, *Evangelischer Glaube und politische Verantwortung. Martin Luther als politischer Berater* (Stuttgart: Evangelisches Verlagswerk, 1977), chaps. 3-5.

Luther was influenced by Augustine, his favorite church father. Although he disagreed with Augustine's basic theological reflections, Luther learned from him a view of history defined as an enduring struggle between God and Satan that affects the relationship between temporal and spiritual government on earth. Augustine's distinction between the City of God (*civitas Dei*) and the earthly city (*civitas terrena*) provided the model for Luther's doctrine of the two kingdoms. But, unlike Augustine, Luther focused on what Heinrich Bornkamm has called the three dimensional character of these two kingdoms: 1) the relationship between church and state, that is, the relationship between the authority of bishops and that of secular princes as it evolved in the Middle Ages; 2) the relationship between the spiritual and the temporal, that is, between the kingdom of Christ and the kingdom of the world; and 3) the activity of every Christian on his own behalf and on behalf of others. These three dimensions are but apsects of the one problem with which Luther wrestled: the relationship between the gospel and world order. To this extent, Luther went far beyond Augustine.[10]

On the other hand, Luther shared Augustine's view that history is moving quickly toward the second coming of Christ; he also shared the expectation of an imminent end of the world prevalent in his own time. He therefore interpreted the turbulent events of his day as trials and tribulations of the final age prophesied in Holy Scripture. He felt that, like Noah, he had to raise a prophetic voice in the midst of the confusing flood of events in which Satan was engaging in a final assault of Christendom.[11]

Luther was also exposed to the ideas of William of Occam, whose political reflections had a decisive influence on the late Middle Ages. But Occam's influence on Luther's view of the relationship between church and state is more difficult to assess. Late medieval reflection on the nature and function of political authority in state and church certainly included Occam's advocacy of resistance to a heretical pope, as well as his insistence on a strict separation of secular and spiritual governments.[12]

---

[10]See Heinrich Bornkamm, *Luther's Doctrine of the Two Kingdoms*, 16. For a concise and persuasive summary of the differences between Luther and Augustine see ibid. chap. 5, pp. 19-28.

[11]Luther viewed the Reformation as Germany's finest hour before the end-time. He even assumed that the chronological distance between Adam's death and Noah's birth was about the same as between John Hus's death and his own birth, 126 years. See "Reckoning of the Years of the World (Supputatio annorum mundi), 1541," *WA* 53: 40. Actually, the chronological distance is 68 years (Hus died in 1415 and Luther was born in 1483). See also John M. Headley, *Luther's View of Church History* (New Haven: Yale University Press, 1963), 240-44. The attempt has been made to view Luther's life and work as a reaction to the imminent end of the world. See Heiko A. Oberman, *Luther: Mensch zwischen Gott und Satan* (Berlin: Severin and Siedler, 1982).

[12]See the section "Action against a Heretical Pope" in Arthur S. Mcgrade, *The Political Thought of William of Occam. Personal and Institutional Principles*, Cambridge Studies in Medieval Life and Thought, 3d ser., vol. 7 (Cambridge: Cambridge University Press, 1974), 68-71. On the separation of spiritual and secular governments, see ibid., 216-20.

Still, Luther's basic premise for his doctrine of the two kingdoms is neither Augustinian nor Occamist. It was distinctly his own decisive insight into the meaning of Paul's phrase "the righteousness of God" (*iustitia Dei*) in Rom. 1:17: one is saved by being right with God; and one is right with God when one puts complete trust in the gospel of Jesus Christ, the only mediator of salvation. Put negatively: no human effort can appease God and thus earn a right relationship with Him; that relationship is only established through complete trust in the word, "the first and chief article" of Christianity, that Jesus "was put to death for our trespasses and raised again for our justification" (Rom. 4:25). This is the article of faith that cannot be compromised.[13]

Luther elaborated this basic premise in a variety of ways in various situations. His doctrine of the two kingdoms is anchored in this premise; it is an attempt to distinguish properly between the world and the kingdom of God promised in Christ, but to see both governed by the will of God, who disclosed His love for humankind in both kingdoms.

Luther's writings about temporal authority (*Obrigkeit*), by which he meant individual rulers, disclose three salient features: 1) his conviction that the state is divinely instituted to keep the world from falling into chaos; 2) his observation that there is great need for justice in the world; and 3) his claim that one has the right to resist tyranny.[14]

1. *The State as Guardian Against Chaos.* Luther contended that rulers exercise their authority in a world which is a battleground between two elemental forces: God's power, exemplified by the demand of the First Commandment of the Decalogue, "I am your God; have no other gods"; and the mysterious power of Satan—a "fallen angel" still under the control of the "hidden god"—who in the form of a serpent (according to Gen. 3:5) tempts human beings "to be like God."[15] Luther refused to dissolve the mystery of this struggle between God and Satan. He rejected the assumption that since God is in charge of both good and evil all of life is predetermined; and he rejected the claim that God has endowed human nature with the freedom to decide for or against divine power. He simply asserted that humankind is mysteriously caught in this struggle between good and evil and that human will—the center of personal life—is at all times like a beast of burden ridden either by God or by Satan.[16]

---

[13]See the Preface to the "Complete Edition of Luther's Latin Writings, 1545," *WA* 54: 185.3-186.16; *LW* 34: 336-37, and "Luther's Smalkald Articles, 1537," *The Book of Concord*, ed. and tr. Theodore G. Tappert (Philadelphia: Fortress Press, 1959), 292: 1, 5. Hereafter cited *BC*.

[14]See also Eric W. Gritsch, *Martin—God's Court Jester: Luther in Retrospect* (Philadelphia: Fortress Press, 1983), chap. 6 on "Christ and Caesar."

[15]See Luther's interpretation of the First Commandment in The Large Catechism, 1529: sin is idolatry, "to wrest heaven from God. . . and setting up ourselves as God." *BC* 367: 22, 23. German text in *Die Bekenntnisschriften der evangelisch-lutherischen Kirche*, 3d ed., rev. (Göttingen: Vandenhoeck & Ruprecht, 1930), 565. Hereafter cited *BS*.

[16]"The Bondage of the Will, 1525," *WA* 18: 635.17-22; *LW* 33: 65-66.

According to Luther, in the First Commandment God demands that one must not trust in any other God; and in Jesus Christ He disclosed His promise to establish a never-ending relationship with those who trust Him as the Father of Christ. Luther declared that the *political* implications of the First Commandment are in the Fourth Commandment, "Honor your father and mother," since this commandment includes honoring of and obedience to the state, which was instituted by God to exercise parental control over the children of this world.[17] Thus the state exercises a divine ministry, namely the enforcement of laws designed to prevent confusion between the human and the divine realms. Every time human beings are tempted to be their own God, they run into laws which show them that they are only self-righteous sinners. This is how God keeps human creatures in their place. In this sense, "law reveals sin (Rom. 3:20)," and to reveal sin is the basic function of law.

However, Luther was aware of the clear and present danger that political rulers may themselves succumb to the temptation to be like God. This is the reason for Luther's constant complaint that a truly Christian prince is "a mighty rare bird."[18] As he said in 1530, commenting on Rom. 13:4 ("he [the ruler] is God's servant for your good"):

> For where there is no government, or where government is not held in honor, there can be no peace. Where there is no peace, no one can keep his life or anything else, in the face of another's outrage, thievery, robbery, violence, and wickedness. Much less will there be room to teach God's Word and to rear children in the fear of God (Eph. 6:4). . . . But God Himself will punish wicked rulers and impose statutes and laws upon them. He will be Judge and Master over them. He will find them out, better than anyone else can, as indeed He has done since the begining of the world.[19]

2. *The Need for Justice.* Luther's basic theological orientation was grounded in the conviction that human reason must be used to discern God's work in history (understood by Luther as salvation history) rather than speculating about the being of God beyond history. "Things above us are no business of ours," he told Erasmus in 1525, during the famous debate on the bondage and freedom of the will.[20] Once reason is liberated from the burden of ontological speculation and becomes "historical reason," as it were, its full power can be directed to the problems of this world.

[17]"We have three kinds of fathers presented in this [fourth] commandment: fathers by blood, fathers of a household, and fathers of the nation." Such teaching became normative when Luther's catechisms were included in the Lutheran Confessions. "Large Catechism, 1529," *BC* 387: 158; *BS* 601.

[18]"Temporal Authority: To What Extent It Should Be Obeyed," 1523, *WA* 11: 267.30; *LW* 45: 113. [19]"Commentary on Psalm 82, 1530," *WA* 31/1: 192.21-25; 193.3-6; *LW* 13: 44-45.

[20]"The Bondage of the Will," 1525, *WA* 18: 685.6-7; *LW* 33: 139.

But the principal problem of the world is the need for justice in the face of the ever-present danger of injustice. Luther viewed the state not only as the guardian against chaos, but also as the source of justice. He was committed to the Aristotelian ethical proposition that human life must be normed by equity, that is, by justice (from the Greek *epieikeia*). Human reason is the chief instrument in the search for and the realization of justice. According to Luther, political authorities must provide just laws to curb the arrogance of political self-righteousness. A wise and just ruler, he declared, exhibits four basic characteristics: devotion to his subjects; vigilance against abusive political power; punishment of evildoers; and faith in God, the ruler of all rulers.[21] Needless to say, faith in God is the most important, since it guards against faith in anything or anyone else and thus prevents self-righteousness.

Luther assumed that even war can be a means to attain justice, provided that it is a "just war." He defined "just war" as defense against aggressors to protect the oppressed.[22] However, he warned against using war and violence to impose faith in God or to establish religion in general. The state can only guard against the worst injustices; and war is, at best, a penitential act which acknowledges that the use of force is the last resort of human rationality. Nevertheless, Luther was committed to the preservation of a Christian society safeguarded by a symbiotic relationship between church and state. The ideal ruler was one who advocated the cooperation between church and state to attain the best possible life for the citizens in a world which is constantly threatened by the chaos of sin, evil, and death. Praising King David as the ideal ruler, Luther, in his exposition of Psalm 101 in 1534, declared:

> The spiritual government or authority should direct the people vertically toward God that they may do right and be saved; just so the secular government should direct the people horizontally toward one another, seeing to it that body, property, honor, wife, child, house, home, and all manner of goods remain in peace and security and are blessed on earth. God wants the government of the

---

[21]"Temporal Authority," 1523, *WA* 11: 273.7-8; *LW* 45: 120, *WA* 11: 274.7-9. *LW* 45: 121, *WA* 11: 276.6; *LW* 45: 123, *WA* 11: 278.14-15; *LW* 45: 126. Luther's use of Aristotle's notion of "justice" (*epieikeia*) does not mean that he agreed with Aristotle's philosophical and theological presuppositions. Generally, he was quite opposed to Aristotle. At times, he used Aristotelian terminology to refute Aristotle. See the sketch of Luther's anthropology by Gerhard Ebeling, "Das Leben–Fragment und Vollendung: Luthers Auffasung vom Menschen im Verhältnis zur Scholastik und Renaissance," *Zeitschrift für Theologie und Kirche* 72 (1975): 315. On other uses of *epieikeia* in Luther's reflections on justice see Paul Althaus, *The Ethics of Martin Luther*, tr. Robert C. Schultz (Philadelphia: Fortress Press, 1972), 135. German edition 1965. The latest account of "Luther and Aristotle" is not satisfactory. See Rolf Schäfer's very brief sketch in "Aristoteles/ Aristotelismus V" in *Theologische Realenzyklopädie*, eds. Gerhard Krause and Gerhard Müller (Berlin: DeGruyter, 1976-), 789-91.

[22]"Whether Soldiers, Too, Can Be Saved," 1526, *WA* 19: 648.1-6; *LW* 46: 121.

world to be a symbol of true salvation and of His kingdom of heaven, like a pantomime or a mask.[23]

3. *The Right to Resist Tyranny*. Luther's attitude towards resistance is another neuralgic topic in Luther research.[24] It must be noted at the outset that Luther opposed any and all notions of revolution in the modern sense of "common folk" revolting against their political tyrants. The only resistance Luther could envisage was that of one political authority opposing another for the sake of justice. If, for example, pope and emperor were to invade Saxony, then Saxon rulers would have the right to resist by force. However, if Saxon peasants rebelled against their feudal landlords they would be seditious and must be punished as criminals. Peasants have no legitimate or divinely ordained authority to rebel. Thus Luther's view of resistance is severely limited by his assumption that only legitimate political authorities have any right to resist.

Nevertheless, Luther did make exceptions: individuals may resist a political tyrant when that tyrant demands their soul, as it were, by attempting to control their conscience. When a state demands to be honored as the source of all power—as a god—this demand is a violation of the First Commandment, and Christians are required to obey instead the apostolic injunction, "You must obey God more than human beings" (Acts 5:29).[25] But Luther insisted that the injunction applies only to individual and passive resistance, not to communal or active opposition. One should maintain one's passive resistance until death against any tyrant who wants to be a god and who persecutes those who do not agree. As Luther put it in 1542 in his lectures on Genesis:

> If the government tolerates me when I teach the Word, I hold it in honor and regard it with all respect as my superior. But if it says, "Deny God; cast the Word aside," then I no longer acknowledge it as the government. In the same way, one must render obedience to one's parents. . . . God wants us to deny ourselves and our life in the Second Table if it is contrary to the First [the first three commandments of the Decalogue]. But if they are in agreement, then reverence for parents is reverence for God. If, on the other hand, they conflict with each other, then an exception is necessary.[26]

[23]"Commentary on Psalm 101," 1534, *WA* 51: 241.27-31; *LW* 13: 197.

[24]See Eric W. Gritsch, "Luther and Violence: Reappraisal of a Neuralgic Theme," *The Sixteenth Century Journal* 3 (1972): 37-55; and Cynthia G. Shoenberger, "Luther and the Justifiability of Resistance to Legitimate Authority," *Journal of the History of Ideas* 40 (1979): 3-20. Collection of texts in Heinz Scheible, ed., *Das Widerstandsrecht als Problem der deutschen Protestanten 1523-46* (Gütersloh: Mohn, 1969).

[25]"Temporal Authority," 1523, *WA* 11: 266.32-267.13; *LW* 45: 111-12.

[26]"Lectures on Genesis," 1542, *WA* 43: 507.13-23; *LW* 5: 114-15.

When it became apparent to Luther that pope and emperor might use military force against Lutheran territories, he declared that Saxony had a God-given right to defend itself.[27] Luther's notion of individual and communal resistance was conditioned by his uncritical attitude towards princely authorities; he simply assumed that every ruler possesses the divinely ordained authority to preserve law and order. This meant that peasants and other common folk were dependent on the feudal landlords they served when seeking liberation from oppression. When Luther was subjected to the evils of ecclesiastical tyranny, he called on secular princes, on the basis of their baptism, to become emergency bishops (*Notbischöfe*) to protect believers.[28] But he never called on faithful ecclesiastical rulers to become emergency princes (*Notprinzen*) to protect the victims of political oppression. Thus Luther granted much more power to the state than to the church.

But Luther did not naively sanction the princely control of religion in territories, even though he agreed with Elector John who advocated Lutheran uniformity in Saxony in 1527 and threatened dissenters with exile.[29] After years of experience with the rule of princes as emergency bishops, Luther became quite critical of territorial church orders that permitted total state control over the church. When it was imposed in ducal Saxony in 1543, Luther openly opposed the government, calling its control over the church "satanic."[30] But Luther could not prevent the development of princely political and religious absolutism in Lutheran territories. State control of the church was established in the Peace of Augsburg in 1555 with the declaration that "he who rules the region determines its religion (*cuius regio, eius religio*)."

The Propagation of Luther's View

Any investigation of the ramifications of Luther's view of the state in post-Reformation history must note the differences between Luther and Lutheranism on the one hand, and between sixteenth-century politics and the modern state on the other. Luther's world considered both church and state to be under God's unquestioned rule. Later Lutherans lived in a secularized modern state, that is, a state which was defined by human purpose and need rather than God's commandments.

---

[27]In a 1538 Opinion (*Gutachten*) signed by Luther and other Wittenberg theologians. See Scheible, *Das Widerstandsrecht als Problem der deutschen Protestanten 1523-46*, No. 21, p. 94.

[28]"To the Christian Nobility of the German Nation," 1520, *WA* 6: 408.11-15; *LW* 44: 129.

[29]See Hajo Holborn, Vol. 1 of *A History of Modern Germany: The Reformation* (London: Eyre and Spottiswoode, 1965), 187.

[30]"Letter of October 22, 1543 to the superintendent (bishop) of Dresden, Daniel Geiser," *WA.BR.* 10.436. No. 3930. There was a real struggle in that part of Saxony about the relationship of church and state, even though in the end the rule of the Peace of Augsburg triumphed. See Heinrich Bornkamm, "Das Ringen reformatorischer Motive in den Anfängen der sächsischen Kirchenverfassung," *Archiv für Reformationsgeschichte* 41 (1948): 93-115.

Some historians have blamed the development towards the modern state on Luther, arguing that he destroyed the medieval synthesis between church and state.[31] But there is a convergence—if not a consensus—among historians that its roots can instead be traced to the philosophy of the Enlightenment, which saw the state grounded in human reason rather than in divine revelation. The Lutheran jurist and theologian Samuel Pufendorf (1632-94) tried to combine Reformation and Enlightenment ideas by arguing that the state is based on rational natural law and should therefore enforce tolerance towards all religious points of view. In this sense, Pufendorf echoed Luther's notion that the state should not violate freedom of conscience by forcefully imposing a religion.[32]

Such early exponents of the Enlightenment as Pufendorf made no direct references to Luther when arguing for religious liberty; others, like Roger Williams (ca. 1604-83) did. He reminded the politicians of his time that Luther and the forerunners of the Reformation, especially Hussites and Wyclifites, championed the idea that the power of the state must be limited to worldly affairs. According to Williams, there is a definite connection between freedom of conscience and Luther's distinction between the spiritual and temporal realms: conscience must remain free, and the state is not permitted to interfere with spiritual matters.[33]

The variety of interpretations of Luther's view of the state in the post-Reformation period reflected the variety of Luther images. There was the seventeenth-century orthodox Luther, whom German Lutherans considered the source of pure doctrine and the propagator of a territorial Christianity governed by Christian moral laws. Lutheran eighteenth-century Pietists opposed to Lutheran Orthodoxy depicted Luther as the model of the godly life and the source of an individualistic religion of the heart rather than a religion of the head. The philosophers of romanticism and German idealism saw Luther as the architect of a patriotism based on the free pursuit of ideas who opposed Roman Catholic spiritual tyranny. As John G. Herder put it in 1792:

> Luther was a great patriot. He has long been recognized as the teacher of the German nation, indeed, as the one who helped

[31]See, for exmaple, Harold J. Laski, *Authority in the Modern State* (Hamden: Archon Books, 1968; reprint of 1946 ed.), 21.

[32]This is the basic argument in *The Law of Nature and Nations*, tr. Bail Kennet (London, 1749; Gettysburg Seminary Library), esp. Book 7, "Of Causes and Motives Inducing Men to Establish Civil Societies." For a sketch of Pufendorf's life and thought see H. Holwein, "Pufendorf," in *Die Religion in Geschichte und Gegenwart*, 3d ed. rev., 6 vols., ed. Kurt Galling (Tübingen: Mohr, 1957-62), 5: 721. Hereafter cited *RGG*.

[33]The link between Luther and Williams has been analyzed by Karl Dietrich Erdmann, *Roger Williams: Das Abenteuer der Freiheit*, Veröffentlichungen der Schleswig-Holsteinischen Universitätsgesellschaft, Neue Folge 46 (Kiel: Ferdinand Hirt, 1967), 23. Williams's reference to "Luther's Reformation" is in the Preface to "The Bloody Tenet Yet More Bloody," *The Complete Writings*, 7 Vols. (New York: Russell and Russell, 1963), 4, 19-20.

reform all of enlightened Europe. Even those nations which do not accept his religious propositions enjoy the fruits of his Reformation. Like a true Hercules, he attacked the spiritual despotism which undermines or dissolves all free wholesome thinking; and he returned whole nations to the use of reason in religious matters, the most difficult feat of all.[34]

In 1815, after the defeat of Napoleon, the Congress of Vienna rearranged the political power structure in Europe. At that time German nationalists advocating "one society, one church, one nation" portrayed Luther as the loyal German who advocated national unity in the face of threats from abroad.[35] In Germany and Scandinavia it had become commonplace to consider Luther the founder of the territorial state church in which the ruler of the territory served also as the chief bishop (*summus episcopus*). What Luther had advocated as an emergency measure in the 1520s had now become regularized. The "emergency" lasted in Germany until 1918, when the authority of territorial princes (*Landesfürsten*) was abolished. However, the German Evangelical Church Federation which succeeded the territorial church was still based on Luther's view that church and state should cooperate with each other for the sake of law and order.[36]

Luther's views of the state received their most severe testing during the Nazi version of the modern state between 1933 and 1945.[37] The history of the German church struggle (*Kirchenkampf*) during this period is quite complex. However, it seems clear that most Lutheran and Reformed (Calvinist) Christians welcomed the Nazi regime, having been historically conditioned to do so by close ties between church and state. A solid majority of German Lutherans approved of the formation of a nationalist church under the leadership of a bishop (*Reichsbischof*) who would coordinate the intersts of the *Reich* and the German Christians (*Deutsche Christen*). The nationalist church became official in 1933. But a minority of Lutheran pastors, headed by Martin Niemoeller, immediately opposed the German Christians and called themselves the Confessing Church (*Bekennende Kirche*).

[34]"Letters for the Improvement of Humanity (Briefe zur Beförderung der Humanität), 1792," quoted in and translated from Heinrich Bornkamm, ed., *Luther im Spiegel der deutschen Geistesgeschichte*, 2d ed. rev. (Göttingen: Vandenhoeck & Ruprecht, 1970), 211.

[35]The 300th anniversary of the Reformation in 1817 became the occasion for this surge of nationalism. See John E. Groh, *Nineteenth Century German Protestantism: The Church as Social Model* (Washington, D. C.: University Press of America, 1982), esp. 2-6.

[36]See the sketch in Ernst C. Helmreich, *The German Churches Under Hitler: Background, Struggle, and Epilogue* (Detroit: Wayne State University Press, 1979), 69-73.

[37]*Literature*, ibid., 577-600. See also Franklin H. Littell, *The German Phoenix* (New York: Doubleday, 1960); and Donald D. Wall, "The Lutheran Response to the Hitler Regime in Germany," in Robert D. Linder, ed., *God and Caesar: Case Studies in the Relationship Between Christianity and the State* (Longview: Conference on Faith and History, 1971), 85-100.

Both sides appealed to Luther and the German Reformation justifying their positions. The German Christians drafted a platform, in 1932, in which they contended that their support of racial purity and of anti-Semitism "will develop the powers of our Reformation faith into the finest German nation."[38] The Lutheran theologian Emanuel Hirsch portrayed Luther as the forerunner of a German nationalism destined to protect Christianity against Communism and to guarantee freedom in a nationalist-socialist culture state (*Kulturstaat*).[39]

The 1934 Barmen Declaration of the Confessing Church also appealed to Luther and the Reformation by asserting that Nazis must be opposed because they are enemies of the gospel of Jesus Christ which "is revealed in Holy Scripture and came to light again in the deeds of the Reformation."[40] The Declaration repudiated the "false teaching that the state can and should expand beyond its special responsibility in order to become the single and total order of human life, and thereby also fulfill the commission of the church."[41] Whereas the Declaration did not mention Luther's name, his view of the state was forcefully presented: "the state has the responsibility to provide for justice and peace in the yet unredeemed world"; and whenever the state fails to live up to this "divine arrangement," the church must remind the state "of God's Kingdom, God's Commandment and righteousness, and thereby of the responsibility of rulers and ruled."[42]

The Confessing Church's resistance had little effect on the Third Reich. Some church leaders, perhaps under the influence of Lutheran quietism, felt that they should not oppose Hitler's terrorist attacks against Jews, which he had initiated in the famous Crystal Night (*Kristallnacht*) on November 9, 1938—on the eve of Luther's 455th birthday. Church administrators and officials of the Ministry of Church Affairs even reverted to a Lutheran nationalism which, in the Godesberg Declaration of 1939, affirmed "an earnest and responsible racial policy for maintaining the integrity of the folk"—and, referring to Luther, called for obedience to the state.[43]

This interpretation of Luther's view of the state precipitated, in 1939, the judgment of the Swiss Reformed theologian Karl Barth that Luther was a major source for Hitler's tyranny, "the bad dream of the German pagan who

---

[38]Text in Littell, 183. Total German text in Arnold Dannenmann, ed., *Die Geschichte der Glaubensbewegung Deutscher Christen* (Dresden: Günher, 1933), 37-40.

[39]In an essay entitled "Christian Freedom and Political Commitment (Christliche Freiheit und politische Bindung)," 1939. See Ernst Wolf, "Kirchenkampf", *RGG* 2, 1445.

[40]Article 1. Text in Littell, *German Phoenix*, 184. Total German text in Joachim Beckmann, ed.*Kirchliches Jahrbuch: 1933-1944*(Gütersloh: Bertelsmann, 1948), 63-65.

[41]Article 2. Littell, *German Phoenix*, 186.

[42.]Article 5. *Ibid*,187-188.

[43]Helmreich, *German Churches under Hitler*, 234.

has been Christianized in Lutheran fashion."[44] Dietrich Bonhoeffer, a chief architect of the Confessing Church and one of its martyrs, also criticized Luther's view of the state, and charged that Luther's view suffered from a serious flaw in the interpretation of the New Testament. He asserted that the New Testament clearly demands allegiance to Christ and thus opposition to political tyranny, and that this opposition may necessitate tyrannicide. According to Bonhoeffer, Luther had simply confirmed the Constantinian fusion of church and state, and, as a result, had succumbed to "a minimal ethic of innerworldliness."[45]

Only in Norway did Lutherans invoke, and act upon, Luther's call for passive resistance to tyranny. Eivind Berggrav, the presiding bishop of the Church of Norway, deliberately used Luther's demand for open resistance to the pope as the antichrist to justify resistance to Nazi occupation. Luther had justified armed opposition to the pope on the part of German estates with the rationale that the confusion of spiritual and temporal power embodied in the medieval papacy must be viewed as satanic, and that therefore the state must wage war against the church in order to reestablish the proper distinction between spiritual and temporal authority.[46] On the basis of Luther's position, Bishop Berggrav called for open, passive resistance against German occupation forces in Norway in 1941. As he put it before the Assembly of the Lutheran World Federation in 1952:

> When temporal authority (*Obrigkeit*) deliberately becomes tyrannical, then there is a demonic situation and thus an authority which no longer stands under God. Obedience to satanic power, however, would be nothing but sin. . . . In such a situation, there exists in principle the right to rebellion in one or another form.[47]

The debate over Luther's view of the state has continued since World War II. Luther's emphasis on the freedom of the individual conscience and the consequent right to resist tyranny has gradually come to be seen as a significant step towards a Lutheran ethic which must demand "revolution in the name of

---

[44] In a letter addressed to a French pastor in 1939. See Karl Barth, *Eine Schweizer Stimme, 1938-1945* (Zollikon-Zurich: Evangelischer Verlag, 1948), 113.

[45] Dietrich Bonhoeffer, *No Rusty Swords: Letters, Lectures and Notes, 1928-1936*, tr. Edwin H. Robertson and John Bowden; New York: Harper & Row, 1965), 324.

[46] "Disputation Concerning the Right to Resist the Emperor, 1539," Especially theses 66-69. *WA* 39/2: 50.22 - 51.7.

[47] Ernst Wolf, "Kirchenkampf," *RGG* 6, 1690. Berggrav summarized his views in *Man and State*, tr. George Aus (Philadelphia: Muhlenberg, 1951). For the story of Lutheran resistance in Norway see Bjarne Höye and Trygve M. Ager, *The Plight of the Norwegian Church Against Nazism* (New York: Macmillan, 1963).

Christ" when the state violates justice.[48] But would a strong dose of Luther cure Lutheranism, no matter how sick it is?[49] Certainly not. Ecumenical discussions on church and state, under the influence of a variety of experiences as well as the power of the state in the twentieth century, have moved far beyond Luther. These discussions have made it clear that ecumenical Christianity must reconsider the church-state issue, especially in the light of political violence and oppression.[50]

Regarding modern views of the state, critical hindsight must also consider the influence of such philosophers as Niccolo Machiavelli (1469-1527) who argued that religion must always be subservient to the state, which exists only to justify its own ends.[51] Most twentieth-century states certainly seem to be guided more by Machiavellian ideas than by those of Luther. Still, the question remains whether or not Luther's view of the state, after it has been properly "demedievalized," has any validity today.

A Concluding Reflection

One may argue about which particular features of Luther's political ethic have enduring significance, but one cannot and should not ignore the basic stance from which Luther addressed the problem of politics: he was firmly convinced that all human beings are constantly tempted to deify themselves. He contended that whenever and wherever human power manifests itself—especially in politics—there will be the notion of one's own ultimate, god-like authority. That is why he held on to the view he derived from the Jewish and Christian history depicted in biblical writings that all temporal authority is subject to the authority of God, who is the master-politician. Political rulers are His servants, and their task is to create just government by making reasonable laws and enforcing them.

Luther was convinced that his own time was more burdened with the arrogance of political power in both church and state than any other age; indeed, he thought his time might be the final phase of history, in which Germany might have to play a decisive role. But Luther refused to concentrate so much on the future that he would lose touch with the reality of the present. He called on both church and state to train people in every possible way to use their reason to attain a fair and equitable station in life without upsetting the

[48]See Peter Meinhold, *Caesar's or God's: The Conflict of Church and State in Modern Society*, tr. Walter G. Tillmanns (Minneapolis: Augsburg, 1962), chap. 3.

[49]William H. Lazaraeth, "Luther's 'Two Kingdoms' Ethic Reconsidered" in John C. Bennett, ed., *Christian Social Ethics in a Changing World*(New York: Association, 1966), 121.

[50]See, for example, the recommendations of a 1976 colloquium of the World Council of Churches in *Church and State: Opening a New Ecumenical Discussion*, Faith and Order Paper No. 85, (Geneva: World Council of Churches, 1978), 151-78.

[51]See John N. Figgis, "Luther and Machiavelli" in *Studies of Political Thought From Gerson to Grotius, 1414-1625* (Cambridge: Cambridge University Press, 1956), 55-93.

existing order. That is why Luther called rulers the "gardeners and caretakers" of their subjects, the "fathers and aides" to whom is entrusted the preservation of the world from chaos.[52]

Luther was consistent in the application of this basic point of view. For example, he did not see any justification in the rebellion of enslaved peasants; nor did he oppose the Saxon court when it legislated worship and morals in its territory. Still, Luther was not the lackey of princes either, as Marxist and Communist historiography contends.[53] He left the Wartburg in 1522, against the wishes of Elector Frederick, to be with his Wittenberg parish in a time of crisis; and he was consistent in rejecting any attempt to deify the state. Luther remained suspicious of politics throughout his life because it was always in danger of succumbing to idolatry. Politicans, he said, "are generally the biggest fools and worst scoundrels on earth,"[54] but "God will find them out, better than anyone else can, as indeed He has done since the beginning of the world."[55]

On the whole, twentieth-century Lutherans do not seem to share Luther's view of the state. Studies of how Lutheran churches have interpreted and applied the Two Kingdoms ethic reveal an uncritical affirmation of government rather than a healthy realism about the idolatry of political power.[56] Indeed, if Luther's view of the state were to become the basis of a Christian political ethic, no one could any longer dream of a perfect world through better government. To Luther, politics was the daily grind of working for a balance of power which would allow people to lead decent lives, rather than trying to erect the kingdom of God on earth. He knew that if one is called to be a little Christ to the neighbor, one also has to be a little Caesar to the neighbor in need of justice.

---

[52]"Letter to Elector John dated May 20, 1530" *WA.BR*: 326.51; *LW*49: 307.

[53]This view has been somewhat modified in a 1983 pamphlet of the Academy of Sciences in the German Democratic Republic which calls Luther a "moderate bourgeois" reformer living in "conditioned dependence on the feudal state." *Theses Concerning Martin Luther*, 17. For a history of the Marxist-Communist interpretation of Luther and the Reformation see Abraham Friesen, *Reformation and Utopia* Veröffentlichungen des Instituts für europäische Geschichte Mainz 71 (Wiesbaden: Steiner, 1974).

[54]"Temporal Authority, 1523" *WA* 11: 268.1; *LW* 45: 113.

[55]"Commentary on Psalm 82, 1530," *WA* 31/1: 1935-36; *LW* 13: 45.

[56]See Ulrich Duchrow, ed., *Lutheran Churches—Salt or Mirror of Society? Case Studies on the Theory and Practise of the Two Kingdoms Doctrine* (Geneva: Lutheran World Federation, 1977).

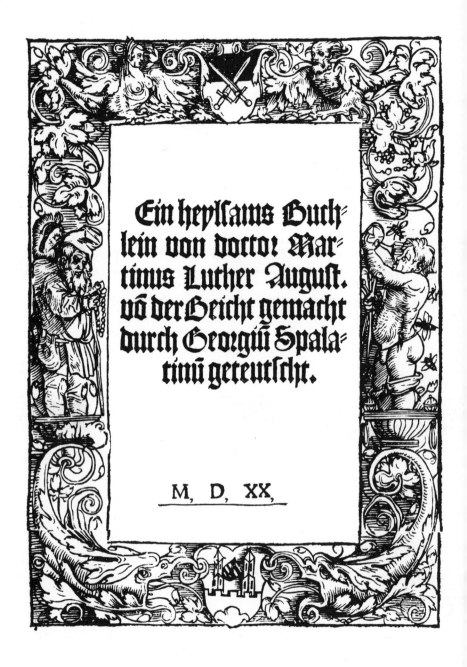

Ein heylſams Buch=
lein von docto: Mar=
tinus Luther August.
võ der Geicht gemacht
durch Georgiũ Spala=
tinũ geteutſcht.

M, D, XX,

The Reformation and the
Rise of the Territorial State

Karlheinz Blaschke
Translated and annotated by
Thomas A. Brady, Jr.

-1-

THE CONSEQUENCES OF THE REFORMATION, like those of other great historical movements, were not confined to the Reformation itself. The Reformation gave the most varied impulses to the social life of that age in all its aspects and began or fostered far-reaching social developments. Far from being an isolated event in the social history of the sixteenth century, it displays a rich variety of connections to the surrounding world. The medieval unity of church and world remained so vital well beyond the year 1500 that religion, church, and theology necessarily influenced, and were influenced by, social structures and social changes. From this perspective the connections between the Reformation and the territorial state are obvious enough. They belong to the well known facts of traditional historiography of the Reformation, especially in Germany, where the Reformation unfolded primarily in a territorial context and with the aid of the territorial rulers.[1] Our task here is not to repeat what is already known but to reflect once again on the mutual influences and driving forces of the two developments, the Reformation and the territorial state. We want to investigate the causes of, connections between, and the mutually reinforcing effects of the advance of the Reformation and the rise of the territorial state.

This study rests on research in Saxon history in general and the history of the Albertine Saxon duchy in particular.[2] Although the duke first introduced the Lutheran Reformation in 1539, the Albertine lands, because they were intermeshed with the Ernestine Saxon lands—the movement's heartland—were involved with the Reformation from the beginning. After its enlargement following the Schmalkaldic War of 1546-47, when it also became the seat of the electorate, Albertine Saxony became the prototype of

[1]"Territorial state" (*Territorialstaat*) as a standard term refers to the nearly sovereign states which arose on a sub-national level in the German-speaking world. They ranged from relatively large states, such as Brandenburg, Bavaria, and Saxony, through middling ones, such as Württemberg, Hesse, and Mecklenburg, down to extremely small ones.

[2]The Saxon lands were divided in1485 between two brothers, Ernest and Albert, after whom the respective parts continued to be named. As a consequence of the Schmalkaldic War of 1546-47, Emperor Charles V transferred the office of elector of the Holy Roman Empire, plus important territories, from the Ernestine to the Albertine line.

the Lutheran territorial state in Germany and assumed the leadership of the Holy Roman Empire's Protestant powers. To some degree the Saxon development also provided a model to other territories, and for this reason it may serve to illuminate the entire problem of the Reformation and the territorial state.

-2-

Political relations in the Holy Roman Empire around 1500 display two distinct lines of development, which had in common only their visibility and influence in Imperial politics. One was the transition from the late medieval territorial lordship to the early modern territorial state; the other was the anti-Roman movement coupled with the demand for ecclesiastical reform. Each development had its own causes and could, even without the other's aid, have endured and attained some sort of goal. The decisive movement for each, however, became the knotting together of these parallel lines through the Reformation begun by Martin Luther. The Reformation came as a welcome event to the longstanding aims of the territorial princes, for it opened to them possibilities for statebuilding undreamed of in the old ecclesiastical order. The most obvious example is the change in the sizes of territorial states as a consequence of the Reformation.

The territorial state could emerge only through constant struggle against all competitors on its own level and against all other possessors of territorial lordship within the region in which it could reasonably hope to expand. The goal was to create a consolidated territory of the greatest possible size, and the traditional means toward this goal were feud, war, purchase, and marriage. The Reformation, however, offered the state an additional possibility for aggrandizement without risking life or lands, namely, through the secularization of ecclesiastical lands. Secularization's signal importance lay in drawing into the territorial changes and expansions some lands previously held in mortmain (the Church's "dead hand"), which in normal circumstances could not have been acquired through purchase or marriage and were protected against forceful seizure by certain religious considerations. The ecclesiastical principality—the possession of territorial lordship by a prelate—which contradicted the Christian Church's original nature, had already been questioned before Luther. Even a strictly orthodox prince, such as Duke George of Saxony, whose relations with the Roman Curia were of the very best, could pursue with renewed vigor and without hesitation the Wettin[3] family's traditional territorial policy, which aimed at the subjugation of the formally independent bishoprics of Meissen, Merseburg, and Naumburg and their full incorporation into the Wettin state. In northern and eastern Germany, therefore, the Reformation made possible what in the South and the West would occur only after the decree of the *Reichsdeputation* of 1830: the secularization

[3]Wettin was the family name of Saxony's ruling house.

of all ecclesiastical principalities and their incorporation into the rising territorial states. Individual cases show this or that formal deviation from the pattern, but de facto the outcome was everywhere the same.

Once the Reformation had shaken the old ecclesiastical order, the three Saxon bishoprics stood helpless before the Wettins' grasp, and procedure, tactics, and opportunity then combined to make them part of the Saxon territory, while maintaining the appearance of the independence of the Imperial constitution guaranteed them. In 1559, for example, the bishop of Meissen had to exchange his district of Stolpen–about half of his territory–for the Saxon district of Mühlberg, of which he received the landlordship but not the sovereignty. He resigned his office in 1581, allowing the rest of the bishop's territory around Wurzen and Mügeln to fall into Saxon hands. The Wettins gained entry to the see of Merseburg in 1545, when the cathedral chapter was persuaded to elect Prince (later Elector) August of Saxony as administrator of the see. Following the reign of a Catholic bishop from 1547 to 1561, August, by now elector of Saxony, took advantage of the incumbent bishop's death to dominate the territory and have his eight-year-old son, Alexander, elected administrator. Merseburg thus came permanently to Saxony. The see of Naumburg became Saxon in a similar manner when the elector installed an Evangelical bishop in 1542. He had to give way to a Catholic bishop after Charles V's victory at Mühlberg in 1547, but the new bishop's death in 1564 opened the way to the see's final incorporation into Saxony. These ecclesiastical territories retained under the Imperial constitution only minor rights of political and administrative independence. The Reformation accelerated in such ways the consolidated territory's development and became thus an important precondition for the formation of the modern state.

The principality's territorial expansion, which in some respects expressed the quantitative side of the state's growth, was matched on another level by qualitative growth, that is, in the functions which made up the state. The building of a territorial state was synonymous with the appropriation and integration of governing functions by the holder of the lordship over a territory, either newly created or taken over from former possessors. The rise of the territorial state thus meant above all else restrictions on the lesser feudal powers, especially the nobles, who were drawn directly under the newly developing state's central administration. As subjection to the state's institutions replaced personal, feudal ties to the territorial lord, the medieval feudal principle yielded to that of the early modern state. On the one hand, the noble lordships became organs of the rising territorial state, and, on the other, the territorial rulers bought up or confiscated lordships and incorporated them into their own domains, making them state property. Duke George, for example, organized the lordship of Bärenstein's lands, which he bought in 1502 for its tin mines, into the district of Altenberg. He and his successors also acquired the lordships of Schwarzenberg in 1533, Lauterstein near Marienberg in 1559, and Dippoldiswalde in 1560, plus Lichtenwalde in 1561, after its holder died without heirs. In 1564-65 the lordships Stollberg, Laussnitz, and Mutzschen were added through purchase. All of them were organized into new territorial administrative districts (*Ämter*), and this policy of acquisition continued well into the seventeenth century.

These efforts to strengthen the state internally were aided considerably by the Reformation. The secularization of church lands, for example, greatly swelled the Saxon ruler's domain without any outlay of money. The great monastic lordships, such as Altzella, Chemnitz, Grünhain, Zschillen-Wechselburg, and Remse, became new territorial districts (*Ämter*), while the monastic lands of Buch and Döbeln swelled the boundaries of the districts of Leisnig and Döbeln respectively. The rich possessions of the Monastery of the Holy Cross at Meissen and of Nimbschen, however, were converted into school districts (*Schulämter*) and turned to the support of the new territorial schools at Meissen and Grimma. The material basis of the state was thus enlarged through the Reformation, though here it brought not a new departure but a continuation of older tendencies.

The territorial state's expansion and the collection of state functions in the territorial ruler's hands shaped the transition from the personal dominion of the prince to government and administration by corporate bodies. Out of the relatively simple medieval government of the prince and his court there developed a central government and administration, which were detached from the prince's person and which became increasingly specialized through the multiplication of their tasks. Following the creation of the Saxon High Court (*Oberhofgericht*) at Leipzig in 1483, the territorial government in 1548 became the central administrative ruling body throughout the land. In 1574 the privy council (*Geheimer Rat*) was founded as the highest governmental authority for important political matters, above all foreign policy and war, and in 1586 a central financial office was established. The Reformation advanced this simultaneous expansion and specialization of the central administration, because the princes' assumption of episcopal functions made necessary the establishment of a new sector of the central administration, the consistories, which were charged with exercising the judicial and administrative authority over the church. They thus became the supreme ecclesiastical bodies of the territorial states. In 1545 Albertine Saxony established the consistories of Meissen and Merseberg, to which the *superintendants*, who had been appointed during the first Evangelical visitations in 1539-40, were made subject. Now the territorial state had an ecclesiastical apparatus comparable to its secular one, and it reached from the consistories through the *superintendants* down to the village pastors. The state thus acquired an additional new function and created special institutions for it. It thereby strengthened itself both functionally and institutionally by using the opportunities with which the Reformation presented it.

During the same era the state assumed responsibility for the material support and supervision of the university and the newly created territorial schools. This sector had formerly lain altogether outside the rulers' sphere of interest and came to them only at the fall of the old ecclesiastical order. Because of the Reformation, therefore, the state became the custodian of higher education. Duke Moritz will always be remembered for having devoted a not inconsiderable portion of the monastic properties to the improvement of the University of Leipzig's financial condition and the establishment of territorial schools at Meissen, Grimma, and Schulpforta. These measures lay, of course, entirely within the state's own interest, for with the intrusion of Roman law into the princely chancelleries and the application of its principles to governmental and administrative business, the training of competent, loyal servants of the state with good legal educations had become an interest of state. The state had also to concern itself with the education of pastors, for once the new territorial church became a sector of the state's activity, the smooth functioning of the clergy also became an interest of state.

The final way in which the Reformation aided the rise of the territorial state was by weakening the state's potential opponents and even, at least in part, eliminating them. With the dissolution of the old ecclesiastical order, the disappearance of the upper clergy, most of them nobles, eliminated an important bastion of noble power. This was important to the rise of the territorial state, which as a whole worked against the nobles' interest and severely damaged the nobility's political position. Organized in territorial estates, the nobles had played no very great role in Saxon history, though now and then they had made themselves felt as a conservative force against change. The rising territorial state could only welcome the opportunity, which the Reformation afforded, to weaken the corporately organized noble forces, which stood outside—and often against—the ruler's own power.

-3-

Any account of the mutual interactions between the Reformation and the rise of the territorial state must consider not only how the Reformation benefited the state but also how the state aided the Reformation. The matter ought not to be seen, it is true, as a kind of planned business deal or a conscious quid-pro-quo, because it arose and developed on both sides in largely spontaneous fashion out of the given situations. In hindsight, however, it may be said that the state's aid to the Reformation allowed the latter to survive. Because the state welcomed the Reformation's cause as its own, it had to protect the movement and assure its future. This was especially important in Germany, where the intervention of a powerful group of territorial princes probably was the decisive element in the movement's survival. It is easy to overlook what might have become of Luther and his doctrine, had they found no princely protectors and patrons. The republican element in the Holy Roman Empire at this time was far too weak, of course, to have become the agent of the Reformation, which could not have been saved either by the free cities and the Swiss—who in any case hardly took part in Imperial politics—or by the Netherlands, with their powerful bourgeois-republican forces. These disunited centers of the republican ideal could never have saved the Reformation against the united might of the princes. The Reformation's survival thus depended solely on the decisions of the powerful for or against Luther's cause, which in the current state of the Empire could mean only the German territorial princes as the personal embodiments of the rising territorial state.

It clearly lay in the objective interest of the territorial state to support the Reformation in order to take advantage of the movement's possibilities for increasing the state's power both quantitatively and qualitatively. Not all German princes, however, trod this path. There were subjective reasons why some of them subordinated their political objectives, remained in the old church, and declined the opportunity to secularize their churches and establish their own state churches. One of them was Duke George the Bearded of Saxony. The sources of his hostility toward the Reformation stemmed not from policy but from his own conscience, influenced by personal and familial considerations. When he died in 1539, the weight of objective necessity brought the Reformation also into Albertine Saxony. Though itself of much later formulation, the principle of the "cuius regio eius religio" was already practiced during the Reformation, which profited by offering advantages to the rising territorial state.

We noted already that the territorial state expanded by appropriating governmental functions. To the rights and power which had constituted territorial rule during the later Middle Ages, the Reformation added the *jus reformandi*,[4] which the territorial princes—along with the free cities' governments—usurped. No one gave them this right, nor had they any legal entitlement from which it might have been derived. It was rather an utter innovation when the temporal ruler began to exercise a power of decision over religious matters (*res sacrae*), because medieval custom had given the king or prince merely authority over the material basis of the church (*res circa sacra*) in their lands. Lay patronage by nobles, sometimes called the "proprietary church" (*Eigenkirche*), expressed just such a traditional conception. In the cities, the city councils acted as patrons in supplying their churches with material support and administering pious donations for religious purposes. In the western European kingdoms the growth of national churches had produced extensive organizational independence from Rome already before the Reformation. In doctrinal matters, however, and in the preaching of the gospel and in

---

[4]The *jus reformandi* was the presumed right and duty of the temporal lord to undertake reform of the church, especially where the ecclesiastical authorities were unable, or unwilling, to do it.

theologizing, the medieval church remained independent from the ecclesiastical claims and interventions of the rulers. The ability of the territorial state to bring religion (*res sacrae*) within its jurisdiction depended on the strength of a still essentially medieval conception of the unity of church and world. Just because the entire structure of individual and social life was so tightly bound up with the church, the state could—indeed, had to—gain control of the church's structure and doctrine in order to increase its own dignity. The state then established a new church government based on its own authority, derived not from the old noble and princely idea of lay patronage or "proprietary church" but from the newly emerging notion of sovereignty, which was founded on a series of usurpations. One link in this chain was the state's appropriation of the right to reform (*jus reformandi*).

The fundamental difference between noble lay patronage of the church during the Middle Ages and the state's authority over the church during the early modern era formed an analogue to the distinction between the medieval lords' ground rents and the early modern state's taxation. The analogy helps us to explain the events that led to the church's subordination to the state. The material basis of princely rule during the Middle Ages came mainly from dues in money and kind based on the prince's lordship over the land. Other cash incomes, such as those from tolls, the sale of safe-conducts, coinage of money, and mining, played a relatively minor role. Under the conditions created by early capitalism, however, the territorial state began to require far more cash than such incomes could produce, so that during the decades around 1500, an entirely new source of income, the territorial tax, was created. The basis for taxation was not the land itself, still tied up in feudal rights, but property, both real and personal, including invested capital. This is why the new tax was not based on feudal rights at all but was derived solely from the territorial state's claim to sole power, sovereignty, backed up with the force that only it could wield. No other power could deny the state this claim, not the emperor and not the territorial assembly of estates (*Landtag*), much less the peasants and burghers who had to pay the tax. The state needed money, and it found the ways and means to acquire it.

The establishment of the state's sovereignty over the church lacked, to be sure, the compelling force of the territorial tax, but it fitted right into the main development in three ways. First, the state found in the situation created by the Reformation an additional opportunity to increase its power. Secondly, the Reformation movement made possible the state's acquisition of a new function, administration of the church. And thirdly, the Reformation assisted in the qualitative enhancement of the state's authority. Had the state rejected the opportunity the Reformation offered, it would have violated the principle of its own development. The thoroughly "modern" (i.e., new) character of this state control over the church, for which there was no precedent and no connection to older institutions, may be contrasted with the medieval view of things with its conception of two powers, temporal and spiritual, which supplied neither material nor formal justification for the new order. The innovation nonetheless spoke to the interests of the territorial state, which seized the opportunities to create the new order of things.

A whole series of monastic secularizations proves that the state church of the Reformation era did not develop out of the medieval proprietary church. The rulers claimed and exercised without opposition the right to secularize monasteries. They exercised this right not just over ecclesiastical foundations endowed by the Wettin dynasty or by others whose legal heirs the sixteenth-century Wettins could be regarded, but also over old foundations by the Meissen rural nobility, monasteries founded by the great noble families, the Imperial abbeys such as Grünhain, Remse, and Chemnitz, and the three great Saxon bishoprics of Meissen, Merseburg, and Naumburg-Zeitz. The power of the territorial prince set itself successfully against both the medieval proprietary church and the law of the Holy Roman Empire.

-4-

We know for certain that in the Protestant territories sovereignty over the church provided the basis for the reconstruction of church order, after the old church order had dissolved in the wake of the Reformation. We may pose the question, however, whether, given the social conditions of the early sixteenth century, the territorial state was the only force that might have taken this task in hand and completed it. Were there any alternatives? One possible alternative might have been an episcopally governed Evangelical church, the beginnings of which may be found in certain ideas and proposals of Luther and Melanchthon, especially concerning the appointment in 1542 of Nikolaus von Amsdorf as Protestant administrator of the diocese of Naumburg. Even if such bishops had been dependent on the territorial princes, this alternative would have preserved the old diocesan organization, which was not identical with the territorial boundaries and which therefore in time might have evolved a new form of independence from the state. In such conditions there probably would not have evolved territorial state churches tailored strictly to state boundaries and thoroughly dependent on the respective territorial states. We must admit, however, that the example of the Swedish state church, which was organized on the old episcopal basis, betrays a development quite similar to those of the German Protestant state churches.

A second conceivable alternative to the state church was the reconstruction of the church on a congregational basis, much as happened in the Reformed Church in Germany. The larger urban communes in Saxony might have achieved this, but by 1500 the village commune was already politically so atrophied that its independent action in church affairs is simply inconceivable. The development of a comprehensive rural lordship (*Gutsherrschaft*)[5] by the local nobility had politically emasculated the village commune, which played no further independent role until the reforms of the nineteenth century. The rural nobility, for its part, which had built its own position at the expense of the village communes, was also losing position in the society as a whole, as it was being pushed aside by the development of medieval dominion into the early modern territorial state and by the economic forces of early capitalism. The nobility could not be expected to play a constructive role in church affairs during the Reformation era, just when it was so fully occupied with maintaining its own political and economic position. The larger cities, on the other hand, lay under the effective control of the prince's governmental apparatus, which made them incapable of any action that ran against his church policy. The fate of the strongly Evangelical forces in Leipzig during the reign of the Catholic Duke George proves the point well enough. In Saxony around 1500 the constellation of social forces was so thoroughly dominated by the territorial princes that there simply was no opposition. This was the state of affairs just at the moment when the Lutheran Reformation was faced with the unique task of reconstruction, and when simultaneously the secularization of properties in the Reformation's wake presented hitherto undreamed of possibilities for realizing the task. In those times such an opportunity could be seized only by the territorial state.

We must remember above all that only the territorial state could represent the Reformation to, and protect it from, higher authorities, such as the Empire, the emperor, and the Roman Curia. The close interpenetration of ecclesiastical and secular affairs, which was the order of the day on both local and Imperial levels, meant that only a strong temporal power could undertake any sort of church reform, and in Germany only the princes had such power. In the absence of such a state, the alternatives—Protestant episcopal or congregational orgaizations—are simply inconceivable. The Reformation of necessity depended on the territorial state.

-5-

In how it succeeded, the Reformation differed from all other religious reform movements, earlier or later. It was the first religious movement in which we may call "the age of bureaucracy" and perhaps the only one that was accomplished through bureaucratic means, though we must not overlook the great power supplied by the masses' spontaneous approval. The earlier Cluniac

---

[5]*Gutsherrschaft* means comprehensive lordship over a consolidated estate (*Gut*) and its peasantry, including judicial, military, and ecclesiastical administration as well as the powers of a landlord. It was the classical social formation of the eastern German lands between the fifteenth or sixteenth and the nineteenth century. It is normally contrasted with the possession of rights of landlordship alone (*Grundherrschaft*), which was more usual in western, southern, and central Germany. Both forms were outgrowths of medieval seigneurial powers.

and later Pietist movements were in this respect very different from the Lutheran Reformation, many facets of which can be studied so easily because the movement was bound up with writing and the written word, the products of which lie in our modern archives. Blossoming in the years after 1500, the bureaucracy of the youthful territorial state took the Reformation's cause as its own, through which it could grow, stretch its functions, conserve itself, and find legitimation. The establishment of the Reformation was in the main an administrative matter, bureaucratic routine in the form of state visitations of the church. This boded little good for the Reformation's religious aims, because it led to the movement's alienation from its human content. The task of bureaucracy is the management of things rather than the solution of human problems, and if bureaucracy is not to be ensnared and overwhelmed by petty details and individual cases, it must schematize, simplify what is complex, and ignore the fine points that make each case individual. Every bureaucracy restricts itself to externalities and formalities and turns the real into the superficial. This is certainly true of the religious situation of the Reformation era, which the hand of bureaucracy made simplistic, crude, and purely formal, as the formal confession of faith replaced the subjective decision of individual conscience and often enough exhausted itself in formalities. The official visitors of monasteries always insisted that those who wished to remain in their convents would have to doff their monastic habits—which were said to be especially offensive—to allow their tonsures to grow out, and to take the Eucharist in both kinds. The visitors hardly attended what went on in the hearts and minds of the monks and nuns, prepared as they were to be satisfied with externally symbolical duties, which they accepted as sufficient evidence of religious conformity. This confessional formalism reached its peak during the post-Reformation era, when, during the crypto-Calvinist panic of the 1570s, the Electoral Saxon state demanded that its servants sign the Formula of Concord[6] as proof of their Lutheran orthodoxy.

The objection may be posed that this view of the Reformation from the perspective of administrative history is simplistic and one-sided. Granting some truth to the objection, still this perspective is necessary if we are to grasp the Reformation's complexity. The bureaucratization of certain sectors of religious life did, after all, decisively influence the nature, content, and spread of the church's doctrines. In many respects to be sure, the way for this development had been paved by the Roman Curia, with its world-wide centralizing tendencies, but it was perfected in the provincially minded chancelleries and councils of the German Protestant territories. The elevation of the territorial princes as heads of their respective churches—"emergency bishops"[7]—illus-

---

[6]The collection of fundamental statements of doctrine ("confessions," hence "confessional") of German Lutheranism, formulated against the Church of Rome and against the Calvinists.

[7]"Emergency bishop" = *Notbischof.*

trates this development, which occurred just as the princes were preparing to delegate this or that governmental function, new or old, from their personal purview to the jurisdictions of newly created organs of government. The growth of governmental and administrative business made necessary this transformation of the old personal dominion into the corporate governmental structures. The prince could thus hardly exercise the episcopal function himself, and he transferred it immediately to the organs, consistories, that emerged in Saxony in 1545. The state's corporate administration assumed de facto the episcopal functions, and an anonymous, impersonal institution took the place of the consecrated, and hence dignified, person of the bishop. Here, too, there was a gulf between medieval and early modern developments. The corporate exercise of supreme ecclesiastical functions reached its peak in Saxony in 1697, with the conversion to Catholicism of Elector Frederick Augustus I, who had formally to abdicate his episcopal powers. These were henceforth exercised by privy councillors especially charged with supervision of Protestant religious affairs (*in Evangelicis*), and after 1831 by state ministers for Protestant affairs, who disappeared only with the abolition of the Saxony monarchy after the November Revolution of 1918.

It was important for the Reformation that a capable bureaucracy took responsibility for its realization, because the completeness of its victory was thereby assured. A religious movement left to its own devices necessarily would leave open the emergence of outsiders, nonconformists, sects, parties, and religious indifference, none of which lay in the territorial state's interest. Once Luther had taught that the universal priesthood of believers made possible a direct relationship between God and man, many types of individual religious views could emerge, because his doctrine could be understood as a renunciation of a normative interpretation of the Christian gospel by an institutional church. In the state's Reformation, however, the mass of the population, down to the last individual, became the object of official religious conversion through the state, a process which, as the sources reveal most clearly, the state was most concerned to extend to every subject. The contrast to the ecclesiastical reform movement of the High Middle Ages could not be clearer. The Cluniac reform[8] embraced in essence only the church's leadership, corresponding to the church's aristocratic character in that age. The reform took hold chiefly in monasteries populated by nobles, it took in the chief spiritual figures of the age, and it became a force of which the German kings and their advisors had to take political account. The movement could claim victory when it gained entry to the Roman Curia. The masses of the population, however, were scarcely touched by Cluniac ideas, and the movement scarcely concerned itself with the masses. The ecclesiastical reform

---

[8]So called from its point of origin, the Burgundian abbey of Cluny (est. 910), whence it spread through the western Church during the tenth and eleventh centuries, reaching its high point during the pontificate of Gregory VII (1073-85).

movement begun by Martin Luther, by contrast, had completely different effects, modes of expansion, and claims upon the individuals it touched. It spread immediately far and wide and penetrated the masses, who became its champions. The movement lent meaning to the religious life of everyone it touched, and its growth became proof of the power of the masses and of the development of the individual. The Reformation movement thus reveals a social situation completely changed from that of the High Middle Ages.

The masses and the individual subject had for the emerging territorial state meanings very different from those they had had for the medieval ruler. The life of the state no longer comprised merely the traditional ruling classes but the entire mass of subjects, who supported the state from their own property. The state needed both the masses and the individual, it required their loyalty, and it demanded from them an appropriate religious commitment. The confession of faith in the Lutheran territorial church was also a confession of loyalty to the territorial state. The state's bureaucracy, with its tendency to level old rights and privileges of the estates and the distinctions among the estates, offered the suitable instrument for providing the state with a religiously unified body of subjects. The medieval unity of church and world thus acquired at the opening of the modern age an application both narrower and more intense than in previous times, being now reduced to the unity of state and church. Precisely at the time when people were trying to free themselves from the custody of a universal, institutional church, they were trapped into a new dependence on a state church defined by its own boundaries.

-6-

We have seen how the princely territorial state exploited for its own purposes the opportunities the Reformation provided. The Protestant princes appropriated episcopal functions, they enriched themselves by secularizing ecclesiastical properties, and they moved with rigid intolerance against the adherents of the old faith. In the light of our current understanding of this development, we must ask whether this apparently so self-serving behavior served objectively a (in restrospect) necessary movement toward the modern state, even though the princes of the Reformation era were quite unaware of it. There did occur in these conditions both quantitative and qualitative changes in the state's structure, and princes must unquestionably be regarded as the representatives and curators of the modern state, which during the sixteenth century reached its first full form as an autonomous institution vis-à-vis the estates. These changes expanded the state's territorial and financial basis through the secularizations, they paved the way for the idea of the state's internal sovereignty through their appropriation of episcopal functions, and they registered, through their religious intolerance, the state's claim to unlimited obedience from the subject. This last principle flowed from the doctrine of raison d'etat. The state regarded the religious confession of faith not as the product of individual conscience—which would have been "Protestant" in the proper sense—but as the duty of the subject to the state.

Wherever such a state did not exist, wherever the state apparatus and bureaucracy were lacking, no secularizations took place, and the people were not obliged to accept the territorial prince's religion. In Upper Lusatia[9] the decision on religion was relegated to the local lords, so that the clerical lordships retained their lands, and some of them remained Catholic in the midst of a largely Protestant land. The holders of local lordships, for their part, also lacked the power to force their subjects to assume one religion or retain the other, and many rural parishes under Catholic monastic lords nonetheless turned rapidly to Protestantism. Given the special features of Upper Lusatia's territorial constitution, the local communities could maintain their decisions against their lords' wills. In one case, the people of a large parish simply abandoned their old church building, once Catholic worship was forcibly restored there by the lord. Finally, in the city of Bautzen, where the Catholic cathedral chapter retained part of the cathedral, there occurred a situation—very rare in sixteenth-century Saxony—in which the individual could choose his religion. The vacuum at the territorial level permitted a kind of toleration to emerge in the Upper Lusatian lands, which illustrates by counter-example just how important the princely central administration was for the complete realization of the Reformation. It is open to debate, on the other hand, whether the pro-Reformation lords, city councils, and parishes could have had their way, had the powerful Protestant state of Electoral Saxony not stood at their sides.

Once the territorial state had adopted as its own the task of implementing the Reformation, and once the territorial prince had nominally assumed the role of territorial bishop, the Protestant subject of the early modern era faced an institutionally unified state and church. Spiritual and temporal lordship were no longer two separate powers, for there was no longer any division of powers between ecclesiastical and lay governments. Because every division of powers means a certain measure of freedom for those subject to the powers, the abolition of the division in Protestant territories meant a loss of freedom. The Protestant territorial state secularized not only the properties but also the entire organization of the church. It subordinated the spiritual to the temporal sword and thereby set the medieval conception on its head. Through the principle of the state church, the territorial state became a unitary authority.

Unitary authority may be regarded as the content and goal of every act of the absolutist state. It would lead us too far afield to ask whether the state church gave the Protestant territorial state a leg up toward the realization of absolutism. In Protestant territories such as Mecklenburg and Württemberg,

---

[9]Lusatia (German: Lausitz) was a province which lay between the Elbe and Oder rivers. It was long a Saxon fief from the crown of Bohemia and was later associated with the province of Silesia. Upper (i.e., southern) Lusatia includes the headwaters of the Spree and Neisse rivers, and its chief cities are Bautzen and Görlitz. It is now divided between Poland and the GDR.

absolutism won out only temporarily or not at all, whereas Catholic states, such as Bavaria and Austria—not to speak of France and Spain—achieved full absolutism without this preliminary stage of the Protestant state church. Saxon absolutism, which emerged fully after 1700, can only be called "underdeveloped" alongside the absolutisms of Prussia and Austria. The Protestant state church was therefore not identical with absolutist development, nor was either the prerequisite for the other, because absolutism grew out of complex roots in social structures, power relationships, and the personal abilities or rulers. We may nevertheless affirm that the unity of state and church in the Protestant territories of the sixteenth century pointed ahead toward absolutist conditions. In some respects it formed a preliminary stage of absolutism, for which it doubtless paved the way.

-7-

The territorial state's appropriation of the Reformation, the course of which we have sketched, quite obviously cannot be considered the logical outcome of Luther's 1517 theses against indulgences. At the outset Luther did not aim at all at a "reformation" such as did occur, and especially not at strengthening the territorial prince's power. The course of events outlined above stemmed rather from the conditions of the age, in the midst of which the Reformation led to the formation of a new ecclesiastical system on a territorial basis, while the territorial state's actions, for their part, decisively influenced the course of the Reformation movement. In this connection it is important that we see that Luther, with his theologically grounded doctrine of the Two Kingdoms, afforded the "Christian ruler"—the Protestant territorial prince—a commanding position both in the world as a whole and in the church. But we ought also to recognize that he was not the author of the territorial organization of the church, which bound the church totally to the prince and the territorial state. He had to come to grips with this development, and probably it appeared to him to be, under the conditions of the age, the only way to assure his movement's survival and to reconstruct the church order. The experiences of 1525, the year of the Peasants' War, which seemed to threaten his Reformation, obviously increased Luther's willingness to cooperate with this reconstruction of the church through the territorial state. For Luther the question of the church's organizational form was doubtless a subordinate one, and in fashioning the concept of the prince as emergency bishop he tried to accomodate theologically to the prevailing conditions. The active element, however, in the formation of the territorial state was not Luther's doctrine but the territorial state.

At the beginning of the essay we noted two developments from two quite different origins: the transition from the territorial dominion of the Middle Ages to the territorial state of the early modern era, and the movement against the Roman Church. The Reformation tied these together. It advanced the construction of the territorial state, while the rising territorial state fostered–not to say, made possible–the victory of the Reformation. The state also misused the Reformation, in that the nearly authoritarian character of the German Reformation made the new territorial churches fixed parts of the established political order. This in turn bound the Reformation to the dominant powers of the age and gave the movement's apparent sanction to all the state's policies and measures. The Reformation could thus scarcely respond to the other social realities or gain access to those parts of the population that were also just then taking shape, though in opposition to the state. The broad mass of the people, which in Saxony, a land early and strongly industrialized, found its political home in liberalism during the earlier nineteenth century and in socialism later on, regarded the Protestant Church as the church of the ruling classes, not as their own. Additional sectors of the population were consequently alienated from the church. The marriage with their territorial state, which the Lutheran church formed willy-nilly as an adaptation to prevailing conditions, brought it no blessings, for the territorial state became the stronger partner in the marriage. Unlike the Reformation and the territorial church it produced, the territorial state was neither influenced decisively by the partnership nor steered by the Reformation in a new direction. Rather, the Reformation movement merely quickened a development in a direction already fixed, so that the territorial state became the true beneficiary of the union with the Reformation.

Although these observations and reflections are based only on Saxon history during the Reformation era, they have some general relevance, because the Saxon case became in many respects a model for other territories and for the general type of reformation from above. In the original homeland of the Reformation, where its first leaders lived and worked and aided the rise of the Wettin electors and dukes, the new forms of ecclesiastical order were also devised. From Saxony they spread to Scandinavia. The problem of mutual influence of the rise of the territorial state and the Reformation is thus not a purely Saxon problem, though, because of its highly developed economy, its advanced social conditions, and its strong princely government, Saxony had a special political weight. The interpenetration of Saxon territorial history with the general history of the Reformation decisively shaped the impact of the Reformation on the wider world.

"Workers of the world unite–for God's sake!" Recent Luther Scholarship in the German Democratic Republic

Brent O. Peterson
University of Minnesota

THE ADDITION OF "FOR GOD'S SAKE" to Marx's famous slogan, "Workers of the world unite!" was an expression of popular puzzlement about what the government of the GDR was up to in its celebration of the 500th anniversary of Martin Luther's birth in 1983. Those who joked, "Arbeiter aller Länder vereinigt euch–im Gottes Namen!" clearly did not mean the alternate translation, "Workers of the world unite–in God's name!" that gave the German phrase additional comic tension. Still Martin Luther seemed an unlikely candidate for a public celebration that would eventually overshadow the one planned to mark the centennial of Marx's death in 1883. In an attempt to explain what happened, this article will examine some of the literature connected with the Luther celebration, officially called the "Martin Luther Ehrung 1983 der Deutschen Demokratischen Republik."[1] Its focus is on Luther scholarship, particularly on Luther historiography, rather than on popular literature, in the belief that works intended for mass consumption in the GDR depend on images already sanctioned by the academic community. But it makes no sense to act as if Marxist history were practiced in a political vacuum. Thus a brief examination of the more public events and products of the Ehrung is necessary before turning to the historical paradigm that has, for the past several decades, served Marxist historians in their studies of the sixteenth and early seventeenth centuries. This model shaped the *Thesen über Martin Luther*[2] which, following their appearance in 1981, structured scholarly discussion and the production of a wide variety of literature related to Luther. Several recent biographies provide an excellent opportunity for seeing if there was, in fact, a *new* Luther in the GDR in 1983, or if the scholarship that appeared was merely a restatement of long-established positions. Assessing the amount of change requires some comparison with older works, as well as an appraisal of the latest writings on their own merits. Finally, to the degree that a shift in content or emphasis has occurred, some attempt must be made

---

[1] The official title of the GDR's Luther celebration can be found in nearly every official document that will be mentioned in this article, for example, in *Martin Luther und unsere Zeit, Konstituierung des Martin-Luther-Komitees der DDR am 13. Juni 1980 in Berlin* (Berlin: Aufbau-Verlag, 1980).

[2] "Thesen über Martin Luther: Zum 500. Geburtstag," *Zeitschrift für Geschichtswissenschaft* (*ZfG*) (1981): 879-93. Also published in *Einheit* (1981): 890-903, and as *Thesen über Martin Luther: Zum 500. Geburtstag* (Berlin: Akademie-Verlag, 1981).

to explain why it happened. No one doubts that something unexpected took place in the GDR in 1983, but without a look at the popular, political, and scholarly context of that event there is little hope of understanding what it was and what it meant.

The official Martin-Luther-Komitee der DDR, which was constituted on June 13, 1980,[3] was chaired by no less a figure than the general secretary of the Socialist Unity Party (SED) and chairman of the council of state Erich Honecker. Moreover, the state made resources available in a manner that was almost unprecedented in the country's short history. Not only were a number of sites connected with Luther thoroughly restored—for example, the Lutherhalle in Wittenberg, the Wartburg in Eisenach, and the house where he was born in Eisleben—but there was a proliferation of artifacts of every sort. In spite of continuing paper shortages nearly two hundred books about Luther appeared.[4] They ranged from serious scholarly studies to popular biographies intended for wide consumption; astonishingly, there was even a high-quality work aimed at children published by one of the state publishing houses.[5] Paper and printing capacities were made available to churches for a wide variety of

---

[3]*Martin Luther und unsere Zeit.*

[4]It is difficult to find a list of all the Luther publications that appeared in 1983, but some of the more important ones can be found in *Martin Luther. Werk und Persönlichkeit, Veröffentlichungen der Verlage der DDR anläßlich seines 500. Geburtstages 1983* (Leipzig: Buchexport,1982). A number of them are worth listing just to show the variety of fairly high quality books produced, for example, Rudolph Große, ed., *Martin Luthers Sprichwortsammlung* (Leipzig: Insel-Verlag, 1983); Martin Luther, *Briefe*, Günter Wartenberg, ed. (Leipzig: Insel-Verlag, 1983); Günther Schulze, ed., *Pfeffernüsse aus den Werken von Doktor Martin Luther* (Berlin: Volk und Wissen, 1982); and Paul Ambros and Udo Rößling, *Reisen zu Luther* (Berlin: VEB Tourist Verlag, 1983). The Evangelische Verlagsanstalt was active with its own program, and it was also able to publish a number of Western works including Roland Bainton, *Martin Luther*, aus dem Amerikanischen von H. Dörries (Berlin: Evangelische Verlagsanstalt, 1983), and Herbert Wolf, *Martin Luther. Eine Einführung in germanistische Lutherstudien* (Berlin: Evangelische Verlagsanstalt, 1983). Admittedly much of the paper for church publications came from the West. The 100 year project of publishing a complete, scholarly edition of Luther's works was also completed in the GDR in 1983; see Leiva Peterson, "Kontinuität verlegerischer Zuwendung," *bbb* 11 (15 March 1983), 197-99.

Another indication of Luther's importance were the numerous exhibitions dedicated to him in various museums throughout the GDR. The most important of them is documented in *Martin Luther und seine Zeit: Sonderausstellung des Museums für Deutsche Geschichte* (Berlin: n.p., 1983).

[5]Gerhard Brendler's *Martin Luther. Theologie und Revolution* (Berlin: Deutscher Verlag der Wissenschaften, 1983) is the most important work by a GDR historian; his counterpart among the theologians is Gert Wendelborn, *Martin Luther. Leben und reformatorisches Werk* (Berlin: Union Verlag, 1983). Two shorter biographies are the totally reworked second edition of Werner Fläschendräger, *Martin Luther* (Leipzig: Bibliographisches Institut, 1967, 1982), and Wolfgang Landgraf, *Martin Luther. Reformator und Rebell* (Berlin: Verlag Neues Leben, 1981). The children's biography, which even includes the full text of "Ein feste Burg ist unser Gott," and deals with theology as well as the facts of Luther's life, is Hans Bentzien, *Bruder Martinus*, illustrated by Gerhard Gossmann (Berlin: Der Kinderbuchverlag, 1983). One reason for the song text is the fact that Friedrich Engels called it the "Marseillaise des 16. Jahrhunderts," quoted in Brendler, *Martin Luther. Theologie und Revolution*, 396. The phrase, as Brendler—but no one else that I have seen—notes, is from Heinrich Heine; see his "Zur Geschichte der Religion und Philosophie in Deutschland" in *Insel Heine* (Frankfurt/M.: Insel Verlag, 1968): 80.

editions of Luther's writings, as well as for other related books; the GDR remnant of the famed Reclam Verlag produced a paperback version of Luther's first complete Bible translation, which included a supplementary volume of essays from leading scholars and writers. One of them, Franz Fühmann, even went so far as to suggest that reading the Bible was essential for an understanding of Germany's literature and history,[6] which is not something that one would normally expect in a GDR publication, especially one that was printed in large numbers for widespread dissemination. There was at least one Luther film and a five-part television documentary that appeared in prime time.[7] Even the Martin-Luther-Komitee was something of a novelty; four representatives from GDR churches served in an advisory capacity to its 113 members, but the latter included a number of theologians who can also be reckoned to the church contingent. Helmar Junghans, a professor of theology in Leipzig and the editor of the *Luther Yearbook*, was the most prominent example.[8] Clearly something extraordinary was afoot here. Western observers were quick to note the anomaly. The *Frankfurter Rundschau* ran a prominently displayed story entitled "Wird aus dem einstigen Fürstenkencht ein Genosse? In der DDR arbeitet die Partei an einem neuen Lutherbild, Retuschen sind nicht neu,"[9] and in *The New York Times* the article "Luther being lionized in East Germany" occupied space on the front page.[10] Serious attention was much

[6]Martin Luther, *Biblia / das ist / die gantze Heilige Schrift* Faksimile-Druck der ersten Ausgabe von 1534, 3 vols. Aufsätze von Gerhard Brendler, Heinz Endermann, Konrad Kratzsch, und Franz Fühmann (Leipzig: Philipp Reclam jun., 1983). See Fühmann, "Meine Bibel, Erfahrungen," 3: 51-81. It is hard for Western observers to appreciate the astonishment felt by the population of the GDR when the government went so far as to publish a Bible; just as remarkable is a statement made by Max Steinmetz, the dean of 16th century historians in the GDR, in an interview published in the central organ of the Free German Youth (FDJ) where he said that knowledge of the Bible was indispensable for an understanding of literature, art, music, in short for the entire culture discussed below under the rubric of *Erbe*: Ulrich Herold, ed., "Luther im Gespräch," (Max Steinmetz, Ernst Ullmann, Hermann Ley, Jürgen Küczynski, Werner Lok), *Forum* 1 (February 1983): 1-31.

[7]See Detlef Urban, "'Ein Genie sehr bedeutender Art:' Bemerkungen zu einem Lutherfilm im DDR-Fernsehen," *Deutschland-Archiv* (December 1983): 1253-55. Helga Shütz, *Martin Luther. Eine Erzählung für den Film* (Berlin: Aufbau Verlag, 1983) was never filmed.

[8]The list is contained in *Martin Luther und unsere Zeit*, 58-66. Some later additions can be found in Martin-Luther-Komitee der DDR, *Martin-Luther-Ehrung 1983. Bewahrung und Pflege des progressiven Erbes in der DDR* (Berlin: Aufbau-Verlag, 1982): 66-67. I count ten theologians on the original list, and I was told that much of the work, particularly in coordinating the state and church functions, was carried out by a smaller group that consisted primarily of theologians and historians.

[9]Karl-Heinz Baum, "Wird aus dem einstigen Fürstenknecht ein Genosse? In der DDR arbeitet die Partei an einem neuen Lutherbild, Retuschen sind nicht neu," *Frankfurter Rundschau* (March 29, 1980): 3. See also Horst Büscher, "DDR feiert Martin Luther als 'revolutionären Vorkämpfer,'" *Frankfurter Rundschau* (June 16, 1980): 1.

[10]James M. Markham, "Luther being lionized in East Germany," *New York Times* (May 8, 1983): 1, 3. A similar example from among the many that one could surely find is Elizabeth Pond, "East Germans busy 'rehabilitating' Luther for his 500th anniversary," *Christian Science Monitor*, (April 25, 1980): 11.

slower in coming. Although Western historians began to read and react to GDR historiography at the time of the 450th anniversary of the Peasants' War in 1975, only Rainer Wohlfeil and a few others have followed the course of GDR Luther literature and attempted to document the recent Luther phenomenon.[11] Yet, even Wohlfeil has not dealt with the latest literature, and his most recent writings have been published as pamphlets aimed at high school history teachers in the state of Lower Saxony. Moreover, these pamphlets were never listed in standard bibliographies or in publishers' catalogues, and they are already out of print and thus difficult for both German and English readers to obtain. In its assessment of changes in recent GDR scholarship, this essay will provide bibliographical information about important, but sometimes obscure, GDR Luther historiography (mainly in extensive footnotes), as well as an examination of the major works.

[11]In addition to his *Einführung in die Geschichte der Reformation* (Munich: C. H. Beck, 1982), esp. 63-67, 169-99, Wohlfeil has produced three works that deal specifically with the subject of GDR Luther historiography: *Das wissenschaftliche Lutherbild in der Bundesrepublik Deutschland und in der Deutschen Demokratischen Republik. Ein Vergleich*, hrsg. Niedersächsischen Landeszentrale für politische Bildung (Hannover, 1982) is by far the most complete, and it contains nearly everything discussed in "Das wissenschaftliche Lutherbild in beiden deutschen Staaten," *Deutschland-Archiv* (November 1983): 1140-58, and "Luther-Rezeption in der DDR," *Themenheft 3. Martin Luther heute*, hrsg. Bundeszentrale für politische Bildung (Bonn, 1983). Unfortunately their publication date made it impossible for Wohlfeil to deal with the most important GDR publications for 1983. He was only able to discuss the outlines of the picture proposed in the Luther-Thesen; Gerhard Brendler's *Martin Luther. Theologie und Revolution*, which was the single most important book about Luther to appear in the GDR in 1983, was released in November, so Wohlfeil could only speculate about its contents based on Brendler's earlier "Revolutionäre Potenzen und Wirkungen in der Theologie Martin Luthers," in Hartmut Löwe and Claus-Jürgen Roepke, eds., *Luther und die Folgen. Beiträge zur sozialgeschichtlichen Bedeutung der lutherischen Reformation* (Munich: Chr. Kaiser, 1982), 160-80.

Other works that deal with GDR Luther historiography include (first those from outside the country) Mark Brayne, "Luther: 'One of the Greatest Sons of the German People,'" *GDR Monitor* 3 (Summer 1980): 35-44. Claude R. Forster,"DDR-Reformationsforschung in der Sicht der amerikanischen Geschichtsschreibung—ein Überblick," in Siegfried Hoyer, ed., *Reform, Reformation, Revolution* (Leipzig: Karl-Marx-Universität, 1980), 167-75, is important mainly as an overview, which informed GDR scholars that their work was beginning to be read and discussed in the U.S.A. Wolfgang Jakobmeyer, "Luther und die Reformation in den Geschichtsbüchern der DDR und der Bundesrepublik Deutschland," *Aus Politik und Zeitgeschichte*, 3 (January 22, 1983): 35-44, points out that almost none of the new views of Luther have found their way into the history books. Fritz Kopp's "Das Lutherbild der SED," *Beiträge zur Konfliktforschung* 2 (1983): 5-27, is little more than old-fashioned anti-communism with particular attention paid to the question of Erbe. Hartmut Lehmann, "Die 15 Thesen der SED über Martin Luther," *Geschichte in Wissenschaft und Unterricht* (hereafter cited as *GWU*) (November 1983): 722-38, is an interesting discussion that will figure below.

For GDR writings about Marxist Luther historiography, three bibliographies are useful: Günter Meyer and Ewald Birr, *Martin Luther. Empfelende Bibliographie* (Berlin/DDR: Berliner Stadtbibliothek, 1983); Ingrid Volz, "Lutherforschung in der DDR—Auswahlbibliographie der Veröffentlichungen aus den Jahren 1945 bis 1980," in Günter Vogler, ed., *Martin Luther: Leben, Werk, Wirkung* (Berlin: Akademie-Verlag, 1983), 521-39; and Günter Wartenberg, "Bibliographie der marxistischen Luther-Literatur in der DDR 1945-1966," *Luther-Jahrbuch* (1968): 162-72. The following people have written about Marxist Luther historiography from within the tradition: Horst Bartel, "Das Lutherbild der revolutionären deutschen

It was Erich Honecker who accentuated the new in his address opening the official deliberations of the Luther-Komitee. After calling Luther "einer der größten Söhne des deutschen Volkes," he continued, "Wir dürfen sagen, daß unser Vaterland, die Deutsche Demokratische Republik, dieses kostbare Erbe in sich aufgenommen hat. Unser Staat der Arbeiter und Bauern verwirklicht die Ideale der besten Söhne des deutschen Volkes im Sinne seiner Politik zum Wohle des Menschen."[12] This may sound like an arbitrary claim on the

Arbeiterbewegung," *Beiträge zur Geschichte der Arbeiterbewegung* 6 (1983): 786-96; Horst Haun, "Die discussion über Reformation und Bauernkrieg in der DDR-Geschichtswissenschaft 1952-1954," *ZfG* (1982): 5-22; H. J. Hertich, "Betrachtungen zum Lutherbild der Gegenwart im Lichte des Reformationsjubiläums," *Wissenschaftszeitschrift der PH Potsdam* 12 (1968): 781-83; Max Steinmetz, "Betrachtungen zur Entwicklung des marxistischen Lutherbildes in der DDR," *Mühlhauser Beiträge* 5 (982): 3-8, and "Das marxistische Lutherbild in der Literatur seit Marx und Engels," *Zeichen der Zeit* (1983): 199-202, (The latter is an extremely interesting article made all the more so by the fact that it appeared in a church publication.); Günter Vogler, "Der Platz Martin Luthers in der Geschichtsschreibung der DDR," *Helmstedter Beiträge: Martin Luther in den beiden deutschen Staaten* (1983): 50-68.

Of particular interest are the writings of GDR pastors and theologians, because they bear witness to the beginnings of a dialog between two sides that for a long time did not even recognize each other's existence. Franz Lau, "Der Stand der Lutherforschung heute," in Ernst Kähler, ed., *Reformation 1517-1967: Wittenberger Vorträge* (Berlin: Evangelische Verlagsanstalt, 1968), 35-63, was one of the first to do so, although he only spent a bit more than a page on the Marxists and admitted that "wir Theologen für die marxistischen Kollgen recht spröde Gesprächspartner sind," 41. Siegfried Bräuer, *Martin Luther in marxistischer Sicht von 1945 bis Beginn der achtziger Jahre* (Berlin: Evangelische Verlagsanstalt, 1983) is particularly useful in spite of the criticism leveled by Günter Wirth, "Forschung und Praxis," *Standpunkt* (October 1983): 259-61. The theologians associated with *Standpunkt*, which Wirth edits, lean heavily towards acceptance of the GDR's brand of Marxism, but the journal is nonetheless critical and contains information not to be found anywhere else. For example, Gert Wendelborn, "Martin Luther—Erbe und Tradition. Zu einem Aufsatz von G. Brendler," *Standpunkt* (October 1980): 99-104, is an example of the extremely positive treatment accorded Marxist historiography by some theologians. Günter Wirth, "Prozeß der Meinungsbildung und Positionsbestimmung. Gedanken um Martin Luther in der DDR vor 1983," *Deutsches Pfarrblatt* (October 1981): 449-52, is also positive about Marxist works, interestingly enough in a forum aimed at FRG pastors; he also contends that some of the early problems experienced by the church in the GDR were the result of its conservative political orientation. Certainly better, although it only treats the early period, is E. Koch, "Wandlungen im marxistischen Bild von der Reformation," *Amtsblatt der Evangelisch-Lutherischen Kirche in Thüringen* 21 (1968): 92-102. See also Christoph Dehmke, "Luther-Ehrung in der DDR. Hintergrunden und Herausforderung," *Themen Luthers als Fragen der Kirche heute. Beiträge zur gegenwärtigen Lutherforschung,* ed. Joachim Rogge and Gottfried Schille (Berlin: Evangelische Verlagsanstalt, 1982); Rudolf Mau, "Thesen über Martin Luther. Zur Würdigung Luthers aus marxistischer Sicht," *Zeichen der Zeit* 37 (1983): 178-82; Joachim Rogge, "Luther-Forschung und literarisches Vorhaben in der DDR im Blick auf das Gedenkjahr 1983," *Luther* (1983): 2-8.

Three articles that appeared too late to be considered here should also be mentioned: Siegfried Bräuer, "Zur Begegnung zwischen marxistischer und theologisch-kirchlicher Lutherforschung in der DDR," and Werner Leich, "Das Luthergedenken in den Kirchen und Gemeinden der DDR," both in *Luther 83. Eine kritische Bilanz,* ed. Claus-Jürgen Roepke (Munich: Chr. Kaiser, 1984), 134-57, 158-76, and Rainer Wohlfeil, "Lutherdeutungen 1983 unter sozialgeschichtlicher Betrachtungsweise," in *Luther-Dekade 1983 Reformation in Hildesheim,* ed. Günter Klages (Hildesheim, Zürich, New York: Georg Olms Verlag, 1984), 49-71.

[12]Erich Honecker, "Unsere Zeit verlangt Parteinahme für Fortschritt, Vernunft und Menschlichkeit," in *Martin Luther und unsere Zeit,* 11-12. Honecker's other statements reinforce the position of Luther in the GDR's heritage, for example, "In der DDR wird die historische Leistung Martin Luthers bewahrt," *ZfG* (1980): 927-31, and "Die DDR bewahrt die progressive Tradition der Geschichte: Interview für die *Lutherischen Monatsheft,*" *Berliner Zeitung* (6 October 1983): 3-4.

German past, especially since it contains more than a bit of exclusivity, but Honecker's use of the term *Erbe* indicates that he was making use of a well-established theoretical argument. It distinguishes between tradition, which might be thought of as the whole of the past as it consciously or unconsciously affects the present, and heritage (*Erbe*), which is limited to "nur diejenigen historischen Entwicklungslinien, Erscheinungen und Tatsachen, auf denen die DDR beruht, deren Verkörperung sie darstellt, die sie bewahrt und fortführt."[13] What is significant is that heritage implies conscious activity on the part of the heir, while tradition suggests passivity. The difference involves the concept of appropriation (*Aneignung*). Indeed, it is the act of transforming tradition into heritage that constitutes appropriation, which might also be thought of as the mediation between passively held tradition and actively used heritage. The distinction has been most fully developed in literary theory,[14] but it applies to history as well. In 1983, Luther, who had always been a part of the traditions of German history, was being shifted into the category of heritage.

One needs to differentiate between the actions of the state, which received a good deal of attention, and the much more gradual development within GDR historiography. It is the latter that will be examined here. Even though the two obviously intersect at some level, there are also periods of lessened contact during which relatively independent development is possible. Thus, while the state may have had a variety of motives ranging from polishing its image both internally and abroad, to generating some additional hard currency through tourism, even to placating the small but increasingly vocal group of Christians within the country, historians, it will be argued here, were

---

[13]Horst Bartel, "Erbe und Tradition in Geschichtsbild und Geschichtsforschung der DDR," *ZfG* (1981): 389. For a general treatment of the problem of tradition and heritage in history see Helmut Meier and Walter Schmidt, *Was du erebt von deinen Vätern hast . . .* (Berlin: Dietz Verlag, 1980).
Not surprisingly, the whole idea of a heritage is thoroughly political; *Erbe* is a weapon in the continuing struggle with the FRG and the so-called forces of imperialism. Arguments with non-Marxist historians are therefore not just disputes within the profession but statements about present day political reality. Most of German history as it is practiced in the West is regarded by the GDR as nothing more than thinly disguised revanchism. See Gerhard Lozek, "Die Traditionsproblematik in der geschichtsideologischen Auseinandersetzung," *ZfG* (1981): 395-98. At least some people in the FRG, if not the practicing historians, also phrased their contributions to the discussion about Luther this year in similar terms. See, for example, Die Friedrich-Ebert-Stiftung (an arm of the German Social Democratic Party [SPD]), *Martin Luther Ahnherr der DDR? Zu seinem 500. Geburtstag* (Bonn: Verlag Neue Gesellschaft, 1983), where the GDR is accused of persueing a policy of systematic "Abgrenzung von den Deutschen in der Bundesrepublik, während sie sich Schritt für Schritt auf der anderen Seite als das eigentliche, das wahre Deutschland herausstellen will. Es geht also um das Geschichtsbild der Deutschen ebenso wie um die Beantwortung der Frage, wer heute Deutschland repräsentiert," 7.

[14]There is a certain amount of terminological confusion between historians and literary scholars, but it is always clear which category, *Erbe* or *Tradition*, is meant to be the more restrictive. A good summary of the position from the point of view of literature can be found in Hans Kaufmann, *Versuch über das Erbe* (Leipzig: Philipp Reclam jun., 1980).

working out the ramifications of a shift in historical paradigms. The new explanatory model, known as the early bourgeois revolution (*frühbürgerliche Revolution*), had been around since the early 1950s, but historians had only gradually seen its full implications for Luther and changed their assessment of him accordingly. Since it was the catalyst in this development, the concept of the early bourgeois revolution has to be outlined briefly. It will also be necessary to look at the changes this paradigm has undergone since its introduction, at least to the extent that they affected Luther's standing in GDR historiography. No attempt will be made, however, to assess the model's validity; whether true or false the early bourgeois revolution remains the framework within which GDR historians view the Reformation.

The early bourgeois revolution, which lasted from 1517 to 1525/6, was a high point in the phase of German history lasting from 1476 to 1648.[15] Its

---

[15]So much has been written about the early bourgeois revolution that it is difficult to know where to start. Three good, critical treatments from a Western perspective are Thomas Nipperdey, *Reformation, Revolution, Utopie: Studien zum 16. Jahrhundert* (Göttingen: Vandenhoeck und Ruprecht, 1975); Rainer Wohlfeil, *Einführung in die Geschichte der Reformation*, esp. 63-67, 169-99; and Peter Blickle, *Die Reformation im Reich* (Stuttgart: Verlag Eugen Ulmer, 1982), 122-34. Wohlfeil calls it a "bisher empirisch nicht verifizierter Erklärungsmodel" in *Das wissenschaftliche Lutherbild in der Bundesrepublik Deutschland und in der Deutschen Demokratischen Republik. Ein Vergleich*, 11, and is generally very skeptical about the theory; Blickle, on the other hand, comes much closer to accepting the Marxist explanation, although he would like to substitute his own term "Gemeindereformation" (86) for Frühbürgergliche Revolution.

Three other general works merit some consideration. Leo Pesch, "Reformation und Bauernkrieg in marxistisch-leninistischer Interpretation. Zur These der frühburgerliche Revolution in Deutschland," *Ergebnisse* 3 (1980): 17-170, was intended to be a critique of Wohlfeil, but it is little more than an uncritical restatement of various positions put forth in the GDR. Abraham Friesen's *Reformation and Utopia: The Marxist Interpretation of the Reformation and its Antecedents* (Wiesbaden: Franz Steiner Verlag, 1972) is one of the few treatments of the subject available in English, but although he is successful in calling into question the work of Wilhelm Zimmermann, the sole source of Engels' pioneering study of the Peasants' War, Friesen is very weak on developments since the 1950s. His simplified view of Marxism equates capitalism with the industrial revolution, not surprisingly absent in the sixteenth century, and demands a mechanical, one-to-one correspondence between economic reality and Luther's positions. The subtleties of more recent works show that Marxist scholars have come a long way since then; taking on Engels by way of Zimmermann is no longer enough. Josef Foschepoth, *Reformation und Bauernkrieg im Geschichtsbild der DDR. Zur Methodologie eines gewandelten Geschichtsverständnis* (Berlin: Dunker und Humblot, 1976) is an attempt to explain a shift in the model from what he calls a "national-materialistisch" orientation to one that was "welt-historisch-dialektisch," 61-101. Unfortunately, Foschepoth's explanation has been overtaken by events.

One could also look at two critical, but still sympathetic articles, which are both more useful than Friesen: Allen W. Dirrim, "Recent Marxist Historiography of the German Peasants' Revolt–A Critique," *Foundation for Reformation Research, Bulletin of the Library* 4 (1969): 3-8, 13-14, 23; and Paul Peachy, "Marxist Historiography of the Radical Reformation," in P. Meyer, ed., *Sixteenth Century Essays and Studies* 1 (1970): 1-16.

An excellent collection of the major articles in which the paradigm was proposed and criticized, along with a number of Western treatments of the theory, can be found in Wohlfeil, ed., *Reformation oder frühbürgerliche Revolution?* (Munich: Nymphenburger Verlagsbuchhandlung, 1972). For complete bibliographical details as well as a discussion of the various texts, see Max Steinmetz, "Reformation und Bauernkrieg in der Historiograpie der DDR," *Historische Forschung in der DDR. Analysen und Berichte. ZfG Sonderheft* (1960): 142-62; "Forschungen zur Geschichte

limits are defined by the beginnings of religious and economic unrest surrounding the appearance of the so-called Pfeifer von Niklashausen in the last quarter of the fifteenth century and the Peace of Westphalia in the seventeenth, which could be said to have ended the period of popular religious struggle and peasant unrest that GDR historians view as one unified, coherent phenomenon. At its outset the period was marred by a crisis involving the whole of society as nascent capitalism fought against the constraints imposed by a doomed, but still powerful, feudal system. The actual revolutionary situation arose in 1517 with Luther's Ninety-Five Theses and the forces they unleashed; it ended when the revolution went down to defeat in the Peasants' War of 1525/6. What was revolutionary was the accelerated class struggle that pitted an essentially or, at least, "objectively" bourgeois movement against the old feudal order, in times that were neither objectively nor subjectively ripe for a revolution. The Reformation was thus only a part of a larger system of events. Yet since theology was the sole source of political and moral legitimacy and the only forum for the discussion of philosophical issues, since the church was a locus of power that could compete with the emperor on an international scale, and since churchmen controlled vast tracts of land and governed numerous territories, it makes no sense to try to separate religion from the rest of life in the sixteenth century. Every religious issue, most notably the question of indulgences, which Luther attacked on theological grounds, was also deeply economic and political; and every social, economic, and political issue—the increase in the number of beggars, the problem of interest, and the election of the emperor, to choose but a few examples—had a religious side. Luther's actions, culminating in his dramatic appearance at the Diet of Worms, solidified a broad anti-Roman movement, and the Diet's decrees had the effect of clarifying the fronts while at the same time allowing the Reform movement itself to become more differentiated. Luther was not ready to accede to a radicalization of the movement, but in spite of him a People's Reformation (*Volksreformation*) came into being in the South, in Switzerland, and in many of the cities of the empire. Ordinary people became actors in a drama that changed the fundamental center of their lives. They

der Reformation und des deutschen Bauernkriegs," *Historische Forschungen in der DDR 1960-1970. Analysen und Berichte. ZfG Sonderheft* (1970): 338-50; and "Forschungen zur Geschichte der deutschen frühbürgerlichen Revolution," *Historische Forschungen in der DDR 1970-1980* (Berlin: Deutscher Verlag der Wissenschaften, 1980), 79-98. See also Rainer S. Elknar, "Forschungen in der DDR zur Geschichte der 'deutschen frühbürgerliche Revolution,' Problemvergleich und Zeitschriftenschau," *Bläter für deutsche Landesgeschichte* (1976): 382-423, and Redaktionskollegium, "Probleme der Feudalismusforschung in der DDR (1970-1975)," *Jahrbuch für die Geschichte des Feudalismus* 1 (1977): 11-64.

    For a recent narrative treatment of the period see Siegfried Hoyer, "Die frühbürgerliche Revolution 1517-1525/6," in Manfred Kossok, ed., *Revolutionen der Neuzeit 1500-1917* (Liechtenstein: Vaduz, 1982), 14-34, or for a much fuller version, Günter Vogler (Leiter der Autorenkollectiv), *Deutsche Geschichte* 3 (Berlin: Deutscher Verlag der Wissenschaften, 1983).

    The mass of literature that appeared as a result of the 450th anniversary of the Peasants' War would also be fruitful, but it was not consulted for this study.

worked in concert with a group of pastors, the most famous of whom–but by
no means their leader–was Thomas Müntzer. Their agitation culminated in
the Peasants' War, which was a broadly based attack on both secular and clerical land-holdings and feudal rights. Its goals were primarily social, if clothed
in the religious language necessary for discussion, yet at the same time these
goals and the people who pressed for their fulfillment were profoundly religious. Although lines were drawn across the old boundaries of occupation and
estate, the Peasants' War did involve a sharpening of class tensions. The
defeat, which came quickly, was not total. The potential for a broad popular
movement seems to have so frightened some powers that repression in subsequent decades, the so-called feudal reaction, was markedly more restrained in
those areas where there had been fighting in 1525/6. Moreover, change
within the church continued, if at a lesser pace, and cultural achievements like
the growth of national feeling caused by the spread of Luther's Bible could not
be stopped. If this appears to be mixing a number of different developments,
it should be stressed that the whole Reform movement possessed common
aims, all of which grew out of the Reformation. The latter was therefore a
necessary preliminary to the Peasants' War, which in turn was its most radical
culmination and the rural counterpart to what was otherwise a largely urban
phenomenon. While it might appear that the Münster Anabaptists fit nicely
into this scheme, theirs was a kind of tragic epilogue that could only affect a
small portion of society. The stage was nevertheless cleared for a more gradual
ideological development that was the real and lasting legacy of the early bourgeois revolution. It included a new attitude towards work, the questioning of
old privileges, and the growth of nationalism at the expense of both the
particularism within Germany and the attempts at outside rule by the
Habsburgs and the pope. This was all necessary for the transition to capitalism
that was being pushed by unstoppable economic developments.

This brief summary of the early bourgeois revolution necessarily leaves
out the controversy that surrounded the paradigm in the 1960s, when Marxists like Bernhard Töpfer wondered how there could have been a bourgeois
revolution without a bourgeoisie.[16] Indeed, a good deal of sixteenth century
reasearch in the GDR has been an attempt to find one, and scholars there have
not hesitated to engage in the kind of polemics that usually surround a new
thesis.[17] Yet, bourgeoisie or no, the early bourgeois revolution model has
carried the day and provided a framework for all GDR study of the sixteenth
century for the last twenty-five years. How later controversies and shifts
affected Luther's position in the GDR version of German history can only be

[16]Bernhard Töpfer, "Zur Frage nach dem Beginn der Neuzeit," *ZfG* (1968): 773-79. The
article and much of the controversy it generated can be found in Wohlfeil, *Reformation oder
frühbürgerliche Revolution?*.

[17]A good example of the search for a bourgeoisie, in this case a fine book as well, is Günter
Vogler's *Nürnburg 1524/25 Studien zur Geschichte der reformatorischen und sozialen Bewegung in der
Reichsstadt* (Berlin: Deutscher Verlag der Wissenschaften, 1982).

seen after assessing the model's impact on the view of Luther that prevailed in the 1950s.

What is striking in the early bourgeois revolution model is the pivotal position of Luther as a catalyst, ideologue, and participant in all the major currents and events of the period. In earlier treatments historians from the GDR had taken Engels' lead and concentrated on the Peasants' War and Müntzer's role in it. This is understandable because they viewed the conflict as a precursor to successful proletarian revolutions in the twentieth century, and it was easy for them to identify with ideas they saw as forerunners of Marxism, namely Müntzer's demands for a thorough restructuring of society on Christian principles. Although a quixotic and ultimately unsuccessful figure, Müntzer could still be a hero. Engels' book on the Peasants' War, written in an effort to rekindle hope among defeated liberals and communists in Germany after the failure of the revolution of 1848, had lionized him.[18] The fact that Engels had titled his book *Der deutsche Bauernkrieg* and not *Die Reformation* or *Die frühbürgerliche Revolution* is significant; his focus on the war made Luther appear in a particularly bad light. After quoting extensively from his *Wider die räuberischen und mörderischen Rotten der andern Bauern*, Engels condemns Luther in no uncertain terms,

> Die Bauern hatten dies Werkzeug gegen Fürsten, Adel, Pfaffen, nach allen Seiten hin benutzt. Jetzt kehrte Luther es gegen sie, und stellte aus der Bibel einen wahren Dithyrambus auf die von Gott eingesetzte Obrigkeit zusammen, wie ihn kein *Tellerlecker der absoluten Monarchie* je zu Stande gebracht hat. Das Fürstenthum von Gottes Gnaden, der passive Gehorsam selbst die Leibeigenschaft wurde mit der Bibel sanktioniert. Nicht nur der Bauernaufstand, auch die ganze Auflehnung Luthers selbst gegen die geistliche und weltliche Authorität war hierin verläugnet; nicht nur die populäre Bewegung, auch die bürgerliche war damit *verrathen*.[19]

Although it has been argued that Engels changed his mind or, at least, wanted to rework his *Bauernkrieg*,[20] it was this early work that set the tone for early GDR publications about Luther. The term *verraten*, with its variations *Verrat* and *Verräter*, is an important one to note, because time and again it was argued, and more recently denied, that Luther betrayed his own ideas, the movement he set in motion, and even the German people as a whole. Two examples from the immediate postwar period show the tendency quite clearly.

[18]Friedrich Engels, *Der deutsche Bauernkrieg*, in *Karl Marx, Friedrich Engels: Gesamtausgabe* (Berlin: Dietz Verlag, 1977), 10: 364-443. For his positive view of Müntzer see 386-92.

[19]Engels, 386. Emphasis added.

[20]For a brief discussion of the shift in Engels' position see Steinmetz, "Das marxistische Lutherbild," 199.

The first, Wolfram von Hanstein's *Von Luther bis Hitler*,[21] is a book that Max Steinmetz, the dean of sixteenth century scholars in the GDR, has recently called "die gröbste und simplifizierendste Entstellung Luthers."[22] In his account Hanstein claimed, "Historisch betrachtet, führt eine gerade Linie von Luther über den Großen Kurfürsen, über Friedrich II und seine Nachfolger, über Bismarck und die Ära wilhelminischer Zeit bis zu Hitler."[23] Yet although the book was approved for publication by the Soviet military government in 1947, and was widely read in the immediate postwar period, Hanstein was neither a historian nor a Marxist. Alexander Abusch, on the other hand, was a long-serving SED functionary who was later to become a member of the Luther-Komitee. Surveying the course of German history in 1946, in his influential *Der Irrweg einer Nation*, Abusch referred to Luther's stand during the Peasants' War as follows:

> Im weiteren Handeln Martin Luthers zeigte sich jedoch, daß der soziale *Verrat*, der *Verrat* an den natürlichsten Lebensforderungen des Volkes, identisch war mit dem *Verrat* an der Nation. . . . Die lutherische Religion diente den Fürsten fortan zur Verewigung der Sklaverei, in dem sie dem Volke als wichtigsten Glaubensatz einflößte: "Seid untertan der Obrigkeit!"[24]

"Traitor" was the dominant characterization of Luther in the GDR in the 1950s. Nevertheless, Horst Haun in a recent exculpatory article is correct in claiming that as early as 1952, in a discussion of an exhibit in the Museum für deutsche Geschichte, voices, most noticeably Jürgen Küczynski's, were heard arguing for a more balanced treatment of Luther.[25] Haun is, however, somewhat disingenuous in ignoring the otherwise almost completely negative portrayal of Luther until the early 1960s.[26] Writings from the 1950s put Luther in a positive light only insofar as he had contributed to German national history through such accomplishments as his translation of the Bible, his music, and his efforts in education. These were the exceptions in an otherwise very dark picture.

The reassessment that started after 1960 was the result of the gradual, but then nearly universal, acceptance of the early bourgeois revolution model,

---

[21]Wolfram von Hanstein, *Von Luther bis Hitler. Ein wichtiger Abriss deutscher Geschichte* (Dresden: Republikanische Bibliothek, 1947).

[22]See Steinmetz, "Das marxistische Lutherbild," 200.

[23]Hanstein, *Von Luther bis Hitler*, 7.

[24]Alexander Abusch, *Der Irrweg einer Nation. Ein Beitrag zum Verständnis deutscher Geschichte* (Berlin: Aufbau-Verlag, 1946), 25-26. Emphasis added. Abusch's death in 1983 certainly saved him from some embarrassing questions about his book.

[25]Haun, esp. 14-17. See also Steinmetz, "Betrachtungen," 4.

[26]See Bräuer, *Martin Luther in marxistischer Sicht*, 3-20, and Vogler, "Der Platz Martin Luthers," 50-57, for a discussion of GDR historiography up through 1967.

which necessarily led to a downplayng of Müntzer and an upward revaluation of Luther. The process was slow in coming, in part because the GDR always seems to have difficulty dealing with those parts of its heritage that are not altogether positive but rather *differenziert*; thus it was only relatively recently that public discussion of such figures as Friedrich II and Luther began. It was also in part because it took some time for the small number of historians working on the sixteenth century to do the research and writing necessary to develop what had been just theses when the Arbeitsgemeinschaft "Geschichte der Reformation und des Bauernkriegs (frühbürgerliche Revolution) in Deutshland" was founded in 1960 at the suggestion of Max Steinmetz.[27] The new picture was beginning to become visible with the publication of Gerhard Zschäbitz's *Martin Luther: Grösse und Grenze* in 1967,[28] the 450th anniversary of the start of the Reformation, but it took the events leading up to the Luther-Ehrung in 1983 to arouse the interest not only of a few historians but the general public within the GDR, and with it the Western press. There have certainly been shifts since 1967, although as will be discussed below, they were not as fundamental as those that had taken place since the 1950s. Still, however they were perceived abroad, these changes were the result of the continuing development of the early bourgeois revolution paradigm following its acceptance in the early 1960s. They appeared to be radically new only because they were unexpected by those who had not followed the course of GDR historiography in the intervening years.

Since the situation in 1967 was already much altered, and since it forms the background against which the newer research has to be judged, it is necessary to sketch briefly the changes that had occurred since the early 1950s.[29] Perhaps, the most important difference was that real historical research had taken place. Instead of merely restating old positions based on Engels, there were detailed studies based on archival research. Much of it was intended to support the early bourgeois revolution thesis, which was assumed to be true, and these early works seem somewhat artificial as a result; but a new, more

[27]See Gerhard Brendler, "Gründung der Arbeitsgemeinschaft Geschichte der Reformation und des Bauernkriegs (frühbürgerliche Revolution) in Deutschland," *ZfG* (1961): 202-5, and Max Steinmetz, "Die Entstehung der marxistischen Auffassung von Reformation und Bauernkrieg als frühbürgerliche Revolution," *ZfG* (1967): 1172-92, and "Die frühbürgerliche Revolution in Deutschland. Thesen zur Vorbereitung der wissenschaftlichen Konferenz in Wernigerode vom 20. bis 24. Januar 1960," *ZfG* (1960): 113-24.

Since the GDR is a small, and by Western standards, relatively poor country, it would be easy to overlook the fact that despite all the attention paid Luther recently only a handful of historians have been working for any length of time in the history of the early bourgeois revolution. They are Gerhard Brendler, Adolf Laube, and Sigrid Looß from the Akademie der Wissenschaften and Günter Vogler from the Humboldt Universität in Berlin, Max Steinmetz, emeritus professor at the Karl-Marx-Universität in Leipzig, and his replacement there Siegfried Hoyer. Gerhard Zschäbitz died before he could conclude his Luther biography.

[28]Gerhard Zschäbitz, *Martin Luther: Grösse und Grenze. 1. Teil 1483-1526* (Berlin: Deutscher Verlag der Wissenschaften, 1967).

[29]The following description follows E. Koch, "Wandlung."

complicated picture of the Reformation was beginning to appear. Steinmetz's *Deutschland 1476-1648*, which came out in 1965 as volume three of the *Lehrbuch der deutschen Geschichte*, showed Luther in a variety of situations, and not just in the Peasants' War.[30] Steinmetz downplayed Müntzer and portrayed him as a somewhat misguided theologian who was unable to appreciate social and political reality correctly, rather than as a revolutionary who was forced by circumstances to disguise his real message in religious terminology. At the same time Müntzer's dependence on Luther became apparent. Not only was his theology Lutheran in origin, but the Peasants' War and the so-called *Volksreformation* came to be seen as the results of Luther's call for reform. Finally, in the 1960s, there were the beginnings of Marxist research into the history of ideas. Zschäbitz was one of the first GDR historians to take theology seriously and grant it an existence at least partially free from the immediate dictates of the economic system. He saw the latter as a conditioning factor that allowed certain ideas success when their time was ripe, ideas that may well have developed in other circumstances. As will be seen below, the position of theology, that is, its relationship to the economic base and to the rest of society, is one of the significant variables in recent portrayals of Luther, too. Still, much had already changed by the mid-1960s.

The 1970s were a period of relative quiesence in GDR Luther studies. Preparations for the anniversary of the Peasants' War claimed the energy of all the sixteenth century historians in the GDR. Luther was no longer at the center of historical interest as he had been in the period leading up to 1967. Except when he appeared in a positive light as the initiator of the ideological, then socio-political, outbreak that culminated in the Peasants' War in 1525, he disappeared as an object of research, which was a lot better than being labeled a traitor. Still his disappearance was only temporary; as Siegfried Bäuer put it in his summary of the historiography of the 1970s,

> Vermutlich sind die kräftigen Farben, in denen Luthers Bild nunmehr wieder erscheint, unter anderem darauf zurückzuführen, daß mit der Konzeption der frühbürgerliche Revolution der Platz des

---

[30]Max Steinmetz, *Deutschland von 1476 bis 1648: Lehrbuch der deutschen Geschichte*, vol. 3 (Berlin: Deutscher Verlag der Wissenschaften, 1967, 1978). Steinmetz characterized Luther's actions during the Peasants' War as "denkbar erbärmlich" in 1960, in "Die frühbürgerliche Revolution in Deutschland. Thesen zur Vorbereitung der wissenschaftlichen Konferenz in Wernigerode von 20. bis 24. Januar 1960," *ZfG* (1967): 123. By 1965, in the first edition of the *Lehrbuch* he called Luther's position at the outset of the Reformation progressive and said that it had made him "zeitweilig zum Helden des deutschen Volkes," 92. But when discussing the War itself Steinmetz still used the value-laden word *verraten*, "Nachdem Luther die Klasseninteressen des progressiven Bürgertums *verraten* hatte, ließ er die ritterliche Opposition im Stich." (1965): 110. Emphasis added. In the 1978 edition of the *Lehrbuch* Steinmetz's judgment was considerably milder: "Luther fehlte es an der Fähigkeit und an dem Willen, sich in die Lage der Bauern zu versetzen," 170.

Reformators in der marxistischen Historiographie endgültig
gesichert war.[31]

One can now turn to the 1980s where it is impossible in the scope of an
essay to deal with more than a few of the more important publications and
a small number of the themes in them. The *Thesen über Martin Luther*
mentioned at the outset will be at the center of the discussion—along with the
contributions made by Steinmetz, Horst Bartel, Gerhard Brendler, Günter
Vogler, and several of the more popular authors. Some attempt will also be
made to explain the reason for the changes that have occurred.

Bartel, the director of the Zentralinstitut für Geschichte der Akademie der
Wissenschaften der DDR, led the group of social scientists from that institution and from various universities that wrote the *Thesen über Martin Luther*.[32]
They consist of a brief introductory statement and fifteen theses that range in
content from an outline of the early bourgeois revolution (Thesis 1) to the
contention that only with the victory of the working class in the GDR did a
true appreciation of Luther's heritage become possible (Thesis 15). What is
significant about the formulation used to characterize the situation prior to the
outbreak of the early bourgeois revolution is the central position of the Roman
church and the failure of earlier protests to change it.

> Nur von innen heraus, durch einen grundsätzlichen Angriff auf
> ihre dogmatischen Grundlagen, war die Kirche zu erschüttern.
>
> Deshalb kam der entscheidende Anstoß auch nicht von den
> Humanisten und ihrem Haupt Erasmus von Rotterdam, von dem
> ihn die gebildeten Zeitgenossen erwarteten, sondern von dem bis
> dahin fast unbekannten Mönch Martin Luther. Er führte diesen
> Angriff und begründete durch sein neues Verständnis der Bezie-
> hung zwischen Mensch und Gott—der Rechtfertigung des
> Menschen vor Gott allein durch den Glauben—einen neuen
> Kirchenbegriff, der die Grundlagen der alten Kirche geistig über-
> wand und deren Struktur und Machtausübung insgesamt in Frage
> stellte. Er verband die auf die Bibel gestütze Kirchenkritik mit
> politischen, sozialen und ökonomischen Forderungen. Damit aber
> war ein ganzes Bündel von Problemen angesprochen, die unter
> den Bedingungen der tiefen gesellschaftlichen Krisen breite
> Schichten berührten.[33]

The quotation contains a whole bundle of, perhaps, unexpected emphases,

---

[31]Bräuer, *Martin Luther in marxistischer Sicht*, 24.
[32]Quotations in this article will be from *Thesen über Martin Luther: zum 500. Geburtstag*.
[33]Ibid., 7.

two of which merit brief comment. The first thing that one should note is the description of the attack on the old church as intellectual or spiritual (*geistig*), or as the second thesis puts it "aus theologischen Gründen."[34] The second is the contention that religious demands were coupled with demands of a political, social, and economic nature. In the middle, providing a link between the two is the figure of Martin Luther, who

> löste durch seinen Kampf gegen das "internationale Zentrum des Feudalsystems" (Freidrich Engels) die Reformation aus. Darin liegt sein bleibendes historisches Verdienst. Die Reformation wurde wesentlicher Bestandteil der beginnenden Revolution, bildete die ideologische Klammer für die sie tragenden höchst unterschiedlichen Klassenkräfte und gab in weiterer Verlauf des revolutionären Prozesses den Rahmen für deren rasche Differenzierung ab.[35]

Luther is thus the pivotal and indispensable figure in the early bourgeois revolution, which establishes him as a legitimate part of the GDR's heritage. What remains for the *Thesen* to do is to explain how Luther came to play this role and to survey the use and abuse he has been subjected to since then.

The second thesis opens with a brief biography, which stresses the tensions implicit in Luther's social origins. He was the son of an early capitalist entrepreneur who was nonetheless still conscious of his peasant forebears. Luther's entry into the university, into a monastery, and finally, as a professor of theology, into the service of a feudal prince meant that he moved into yet another sphere. "Er wurde zu einem Vertreter einer zumeist dem Bürgertum nahestehenden, zum teil frühkapitalistische Interessen ausdrückenden, vom Territorialfürstentum und Kirche materiell abhängigen Intelligenz."[36] In short, after exposure to nearly every level of society, he was torn in all directions. Ultimately this was to be his undoing, but in the early 1520s the question of his ultimate allegiance had not yet been posed, and all his potential allies were still more or less unified. In fact, it was Luther's dramatic refusal to recant in Worms that was a crystalizing event for the whole Reform movement. Thesis IV calls it "die ruhmvollste Tat seines Lebens, Symbol unbeugsamer Charakterstärke und Überzeugungstreue."[37] This was also the period in which he began translating the Bible, "seine größte kulturelle Leistung." (IV)[38] Thesis V talks about the process of differentiation within the Reformation, largely along class lines:

[34]Ibid., 9.

[35]Ibid., 8.

[36]Ibid., 13.

[37]Ibid., 13.

[38]Ibid., 13.

Zunächst unterstützte Luther noch partiell die Volksbewegung und versuchte, die sich erweiternde Kluft zur adligen Ständeopposition zu überbrücken, obwohl er jetzt von weiterdrängenden Kräften, insbesondere von Thomas Müntzer, kritisiert und angegriffen wurde und sich seinerseits mit diesem auseinandersetzte. . . . So entwickelte Luther bis 1524 sein Program der Reformation, das mit friedlichen Mitteln im Bündnis mit den weltlichen Obrigkeiten durchgesetzt werden sollte.[39]

Armed conflict was, however, the inevitable result of the social tensions, and Luther allied himself with what he saw to be the forces of moderation and reason. Yet his writings against the peasants were, in the view of the *Thesen*, everything other than reasonable—even though his decision to oppose them can be explained:

Die *Tragik* Luthers bestand darin, daß er in den Widerspruch geriet zwischen seiner Rolle als Initiator einer breiten, alle oppositionellen Klassen und Schichten einbeziehenden revolutionären Bewegung und seiner eigenen begrenzten Zielstellung, die letztlich in seiner bürgerlich-gemäßigten, auf das Landesfürstetum orientierten Klassenposition begründet war.[40]

Of particular interest here is the fact that Luther no longer appears as a traitor; he was the tragic victim of his own background, which is a considerably milder judgment.

The rest of the *Thesen* deal with Luther's attempts to consolidate the gains of the Reformation, with the help of the princes (VII), the European and world-wide expansion of Lutheranism, along with a kind of "spirit of Protestantism" in politics and economics (VIII), the cultural-historical importance of the Reformation in the development of the arts (IX), and the legal acceptance of Lutherans following the Peace of Augsburg in 1555 (X). Theses XI through XV recap the history of Lutheran reception from the sixteenth century to the present. One highpoint was the development of historical materialism by Marx and Engels, which made a "wissenschaftliche Auffassung der Reformation und Martin Luther"[41] possible for the first time (XII). Finally,

Mit dem sieg der Arbeiterklasse und ihrer Verbündeten, mit dem Aufbau und der Gestaltung des Sozialismus sind in der Deutschen

---

[39]Ibid., 16-17.
[40]Ibid., 19. Emphasis added.
[41]Ibid., 30.

Demokratischen Republik die gesellschaftlichen Voraussetzungen dafür geschaffen, Martin Luther allseitig wissenschaftlich begründet und gerecht zu würdigen. (XV)[42]

A number of criticisms are possible here.[43] Concentration on the historical impact of Luther leaves the impression that the importance of his Bible translation, for example, is to be found in its social and cultural Wirkungsgeschichte. No mention is made of Luther's and his contemporaries' belief that the Bible is the Holy Scripture, through which God spoke and continues to speak to man's needs. Nor is it possible to prove the class basis of various positions that Luther himself viewed as the product of careful exegesis. On the other hand, theological Luther studies have often been accused of missing the historical context and historicity of Luther's thought;[44] the Marxist perspective has at least forced GDR theologians to take history seriously, apparently with no ill effects. Marxists, too, have begun to do their theological homework. It is also not fair to conclude as Hartmut Lehmann did that the *Thesen* present a "gigantisches Klichee von einem Helden!"[45] Theses are necessarily short and oversimplified, and it is unrealistic to expect more from them than a framework or, in the case of the GDR, guidelines for future discussion and research. To get an accurate picture of GDR Luther scholarship it is necessary to look at the major biographies produced during 1983.

Gerhard Brendler's *Martin Luther Theologie und Revolution* certainly ranks as the most important single work produced in the GDR on Luther since Zschäbitz's 1967 biography. Although a popular treatment that maddeningly refuses to identify any changes or disagreements in Marxist historiography, much less to document them in a footnote, it breaks new ground not so much with the factual material it contains as with the unexpected treatment of long-established facts. Brendler uses the freedom accorded to the second generation of sixteenth-century historical scholars; since the history of the early bourgeois revolution has already been written, he can "mehr Luthers *geistiger* Entwicklung und seinem *individuellen* Verhalten zuwenden."[46] Already in the foreword, Brendler claims a "relative Selbständigkeit" for Luther's intellectual development and his resultant theology.[47] This does not mean that he ignores Luther's social origins but that, as the *Thesen* already put it, he sees Luther caught on the border between a number of social classes and concludes that

---

[42]Ibid., 35.

[43]See Wohlfeil, *Das wissenschaftliche Lutherbild,* and "Luther Rezeption in der DDR," Lehmann, "Die 15 Thesen," Mau, and Bräuer, *Martin Luther in marxistischer Sicht,* 28-32.

[44]See, for example, Bernd Moeller, "Probleme der Reformationsgeschichtsforschung," *Zeitschrift für Kirchengeschichte* (1965): 246-57.

[45]Lehmann, "Die 15 Thesen," 735.

[46]Brendler, *Martin Luther,* 7. Emphasis added.

[47]Ibid., 7.

"mit Generalisierungen der Art, daß Martin Luther ein Mann des Bürgertums gewesen sei, ist wenig gewonnen."[48] What this means for a Marxist treatment of the history of ideas, specifically for a Marxist treatment of theology, was recently put best by Günter Vogler, in his discussion of the origins of Luther's theology,

> Ausgangspunkt für Luther war das Gottesbild und das Verhältnis zwischen Mensch und Gott. Von daher entwickelte er eine Theologie, die zwar gesellschaftlich determiniert ist und auf die Gesellschaft revolutionierend einwirkte, aber nicht gänzlich aus der gesellschaftlichen Determiniertheit zu erklären ist und auch nicht in allen ihren Elementen gesellschaftliche Relevanz besaß. Wo es um Glaubenserlebnisse ging, bewegen wir uns im Bereich des *spezifisch Theologischen*. Insofern besitzt der Reformationsprozeß seinen *Eigenwert*, kann die Reformation nicht ausschließlich als Phase im Verlauf der deutschen frühbürgerlichen Revolution gesehen werden.[49]

The results of such a shift of emphasis can be quite startling, as is shown by examining several historians' portrayals of the same event, namely Luther's decision to enter a monastery. Writing in 1965 in the first edition of the *Lehrbuch der deutschen Geschichte Deutschland von 1476 bis 1648*, Max Steinmetz explained it as follows: "Man wird nicht fehlgehen, wenn man diesen schwerwiegenden Schritt als Ausdruck der allgemeinen gesellschaftlichen Krise ansieht, die auch vor den psychischen Bereichen nicht haltmachte und die Lebenssicherheit der Menschen empfindlich zu stören vermochte."[50] Yet while Steinmetz repeated the same formulation in the 1978 second edition of his basic textbook,[51] Gerhard Zschäbitz's 1967 *Martin Luther Grösse und Grenze*, the first serious Marxist Luther biography, had shifted the emphasis significantly. After spending fifteen pages describing the social and economic background of Luther's decision, he concludes:

> Diese gesellschftliche Gesamtsituation stellte den Hintergrund für Luthers Eintritt ins Kloster dar. All ihre Probleme hatten Martin Luther gefühlsmäßig berührt und waren in seinem Denken und Empfinden zur brennenden Frage nach dem wahren Verhältnis Gottes zu den Menschen zusammengeflossen, in erster Linie aber zunächst zur Frage nach der *eigenen Heilsgewissheit*.[52]

[48]Brendler, "Revolutionäre Potenzen," 161.

[49]Vogler,"Der Platz Martin Luthers," 62. Emphasis added.

[50]Steinmetz, *Deutschland von 1476 bis 1648* (1965), 88.

[51]Steinmetz, *Deutschland von 1476 bis 1648* (1978), 97.

[52]Zschäbitz, 52. Emphasis added. For his description of the social background see 35-51.

Societal factors are thus no longer the only considerations; theology and personal needs play a role, albeit not a decisive one. The problem of weighing these factors without succumbing to an idealist perspective that only describes individual intellectual and emotional problems while omitting what for Marxists must be the dominant economic base can easily be seen in Werner Fläschendränger's *Martin Luther*, a popular biography that also appeared in 1967, clearly under the influence of Zschäbitz.[53] Flaschendränger claims that Luther's decision was "keineswegs . . . eine Affekthandlung," but rather,

> Luthers Gewissenqualen lassen sich nicht von der spannungsgeladenen gesellschaftliche Stiuation seiner Zeit trennen. So konnte die Flucht des jungen Magisters hinter Klostermauern, die der Blitzschlag von Stotternheim *nur ausgelößt* hatte, keinen Ausweg aus seinen persönlichen Nöten herbeiführen.[54]

Significantly, the second sentence of this quotation was eliminated from the 1982 edition of the book,[55] which means that Luther's decision was no longer viewed as the automatic, unavoidable result of social pressures. Flaschendränger's new, shorter version admits the possiblity of what Vogler called the specifically theological elements of the event.

Brendler's otherwise clear, dynamic tone becomes extremely tentative at this point, which is again symptomatic of both the change in attitude towards theological problems and the difficulty in dealing with them in Marxist terms, particularly in dealing with an individual's decision-making process:

> Bedenkt man den Zustand der damaligen Gesellschaft, so drängt sich geradezu der Gedanke auf, daß dieser schritt Luthers *durchaus auch davon mitverursacht gewesen sein könnte*, daß er insgesamt mit seiner Umwelt unzufrieden war . . . Allerdings läßt sich keine dieser Annahmen schlüssig beweisen, so daß wir auch damit rechnen können, daß der Entschluß, ins Kloster zu gehen, tatsächlich wie der Blitz aus heiterem Himmel kam.[56]

This shift is the result of the "relative Selbständigkeit" Brendler grants to ideas. In the space that Zschäbitz used for a description of Luther's world Brendler discusses the philosophical currents of the time and the development of Luther's thought. His book thus contains a long discussion of the course of medieval theology from its struggles with Aristotle by way of Thomas

[53]Fläschendränger (1967).

[54]Fläschendränger (1967), 9-11. Emphasis added.

[55]Fläschendränger (1982), 10-12. See also Landgraf, 34.

[56]Brendler, *Martin Luther*, 25. Emphasis added.

Aquinas to the Occamist circle at Erfurt where Luther attended the university, and he even includes a summary of the major themes of the Bible for the large number of readers among his countrymen who he assumed to be unfamiliar with it.[57] Whole chapters are filled with nothing but theology; an appraisal of Luther's lectures on the Psalms and the Epistle to the Romans, for example, occupies nearly thirty pages.[58] While the content of such passages may not be surprising to specialists, the fact of their inclusion and length in a GDR biography is rather remarkable.

This is not to say that there is no historical framework to the presentation or that the effects of Luther's theology are not ultimately the reason for the book's existence and the background for the re-evaluation of Luther in the GDR. Still, theology in and of itself is remarkably central to Brendler's portrait of Luther. His emphasis can, perhaps, best be seen in the treatment of Luther's translation of the Bible.[59] Brendler starts by describing Luther's achievement as primarily theological, that is to say, his most important act was to use Christ as the fundament that anchored the whole interpretation. It was, according to Brendler, Luther's unified and unifying approach that made a free translation into comprehensible German possible. The resultant prose, which became the basis of standard German, was by no means Luther's creation, although no one, not the least Brendler, would deny Luther's genius as a writer. The language's strength was due in no small part to Wittenberg's position near a number of linguistic borders, which made Luther's German understandable to nearly all Germans, no matter which dialect they actually spoke. As a result, his version of the Bible would be the most widely read book in Germany for the next few centuries. The failure of earlier German Bibles to catch on was due not only to their stylistic imperfections but was also caused by their appearance at inopportune times. Here then is the first social or historical component of Brendler's analysis. It stresses his claim that no need for a German Bible can be taken as given, rather that the crisis of feudal society and the fact that the Bible seemed to speak to its tensions—interpreting the Bible became an important locus of ideological struggle—meant that the time was ripe for the Luther Bible. Finally, for Brendler, the most important audience for Luther's Bible was made up of the peasants and plebians who were now able to justify their demands with the new concept of divine (*göttliches*) rather than tradition law (*altes Recht*). Against his will and inclinations Luther became involved in a movement far larger than he anticipated in the strictly theological controvesies he initiated.

---

[57]Ibid., for his description of medieval theology and university life see 32-37, 81-84. His summary of the Bible is on 50-60, 62-63.

[58]Ibid., 48-75.

[59]Ibid., 284-87.

This kind of treatment could enhance the Marxist-Christian dialog in the GDR. A discussion of writings about Luther by the various organs of the church would make this article unmanageably long, but even a brief look at the major Lutheran biography of Luther by Gert Wendelborn shows that it has as much social history as Brendler has theology. Since Honecker's historic meeting with church leaders in 1978,[60] the two sides have no longer considered themselves implacable adversaries. Regular meetings between Marxist historians and theologians and church historians have been taking place since the mid-1970s, although they have not been acknowledged publicly until recently.[61] While it is clear that their interests concerning Luther are fundamentally different, there has clearly been some profit to both sides when measured in terms of research. It will be interesting to watch the preparations for the upcoming Müntzer anniversary because it is clear that the old portrayal that showed him as a political revolutionary rather than as a theologian is inadequate. It is also clear that his theology, and particularly his relationship to Luther, needs further clarification. Just what this might signify for the everyday existence of the church in the GDR lies in the realm of speculation, but again it will be hard to return to an adversary relationship after the fairly close and fruitful contact during the Luther-Ehrung.[62]

This then raises the question of the causes and intentions of the vast number of publications and events in 1983. One cannot be satisfied with facile statements like those from Hartmut Lehmann, who claims that Luther was used cynically to pour "'Zement' in die Staatsfundamente der DDR,"[63] or from Franz Loeser, a former professer of philosophy at Humboldt University in East Berlin who recently received asylum in the West:

[60]See "Kirchen," in *DDR Handbuch*, ed. Bundesministerium für innerdeutsche Beziehungen (Köln: Verlag Wissenschaft und Politik, 1979), 586-96, esp. 594. The full GDR report can be found in *Neues Deutschland* (March 7, 1978).

[61]Bräuer in *Martin Luther in marxistischer Sicht* claims to be the first one to admit such meetings publicly. He says in a footnote, "Im Pastoralkolleg der Ev.-luth. Landeskirche Sachsens (Krummenhennersdorf) fand 1979 eine Tagung zum Thema "Stadt und Reformation" statt, an der eine größere Zahl von Kirchenhistorikern und Historikern beteiligt war," 44. In a conversation with me he said that there had been meetings there in 1975 and 1977 as well, but although he had organized them and invited the Marxist historians (privately, to visit him in his "residence"), he had not disclosed the fact until now because the historians might have gotten into trouble for not having informed their party leadership. In 1983 the change in climate meant they no longer had anything to fear. He also said that there had been some contact between him and Max Steinmetz as early as 1968, initiated by Steinmetz, who found out that Bräuer shared his interest in Thomas Müntzer. Steinmetz himself indicated how different the situation had been as late as 1967; writing in the church publication *Zeichen der Zeit*, "Das marxistische Lutherbild," 202, he said, "Noch 1967 sprachen Lau in der wittenberger Stadtkirche und Steinmetz in der Lutherhalle, ohne voneinander mehr als geographisch Kenntnis zu nehmen." Günter Wirth claimed in a conversation that there had been contacts with more progressive elements in the church at a far earlier date. See his "Forschung und Praxis."

[62]See Bräuer, "Die Bedeutung des Luther-Jubiläums für die Kirche in der DDR," *Helmstedter Beiträge. Martin Luther in beiden deutschen Staaten* (1983): 32-47, and Mau.

[63]Lehmann, "Die 15 Thesen," 737.

> Die Wissenschaft erhielt den Auftrag, sich in diesem Jahr intensiv
> mit dem Reformator zu beschäftigen–nicht etwa, weil die
> Persönlichkeit Luthers plötzlich der SED-Führung ins
> ideologische Konzept gepaßt hätte. Der einzige Grund, die
> Würdigung durchzupauken war die politische Opportunität: Mit
> Hilfe der Luther-Ehrung hoffte die Parteispitze, das Ansehen der
> DDR international aufzuwerten. (Und einiges an Devisen sollten
> gläubige Lutheraner aus aller Welt als Touristen auch in die
> DDR-Staatskasse bringen.)[64]

This is not to say that they are totally wrong, but there was obviously more involved than a short-term, expedient decision. While it is clear that there has been some movment on both internal and international political fronts, it is also true that the GDR is beginning to deal with ambiguous figures like Luther in a much more self-assured fashion that might be linked to a certain maturity on the part of the state and the historical profession there. The above discussion of *Erbe* should indicate how complicated the questions of the GDR's relationship to the past and to its present-day image of itself are. These are, moreover, legitimate concerns–and, perhaps, legitimate fields of inquiry as well–even if western academics, who are suspicious of such theories, usually confine themselves to complaining about their students' lack of historical knowledge and historical consciousness rather than about the place of history and historical knowledge in the society. One could also accept the claim of political motivation on the part of the government without necessarily concluding that GDR historical scholarship is hopelessly tainted. No Marxist historian would deny what Brendler called the "Prinzip der Parteilichkeit in der marxistisch-leninistischen Geschichtswissenschaft,"[65] but he would dismiss the claims of objectivity put forth by non-Marxists as self-serving lies or delusions. In addition, there is often a process of development within the discipline of history on both sides that proceeds apart from day-to-day political exigencies, in much the same way as Luther's thought had its own "relative Selbstständigkeit."

The thesis of this article has been that the changing view of Luther in the GDR was determined primarily by the acceptance and development of the early bourgeois revolution paradigm. And, contrary to what some scholars have argued, it should now be clear that the model has been productive.[66] For

---

[64]Franz Loeser, "Der Rat der sozialistischen Götter," *Der Spiegel* 34 (1984): 113.

[65]Brendler, "Zum Prinzip der Parteilichkeit in der marxistisch-leninistischen Geschichtswissenschaft," *ZfG* (1972): 277-301.

[66]Foschepoth contends that the theory has degenerated into a "Leerformel, die sich methodologisch und inhaltlich zwar variieren, aber nicht verifizieren läßt." 114. Suffice it to say that, in the years since 1976, when Foschepoth's book appeared, GDR historians have not given up trying–I would argue with some notable successes.

example, while there is certainly room for disagreement with some of Brendler's judgments, they are nevertheless a good deal closer to the views of serious historians and theologians in other parts of the world, and to those writing in different intellectual traditions. Although much has changed in the GDR in the interim, Brendler is also much closer to Zschäbitz than the latter was to his predecessors from the period before the acceptance of the early bourgeois revolution paradigm. Much still remains to be done, but the tension within Marxist Luther historiography seems to have lessened considerably. As Adolf Laube from the Akademie der Wissenschaften put it, one of the most significant achievements of the Luther-Ehrung was, "daß eine marxistische Lutherforschung überhaupt in Gang gekommen ist."[67] For the church, for the state, and for the population in general, the public act of upward revaluation in 1983 was more important, and it was certainly more noticeable in the West. Yet, the roots of the change lay elsewhere. Whatever demands may have been put on historians by the state, they were able to meet them without a wholesale scrapping of previously held positions.

---

[67]Adolf Laube quoted in "Was erbrachte die Luther-Ehrung. Erster Versuch einer Bilanzierung in einer Umfrage unter Gesellschaftswissenschaftlern und Theologen," *Standpunkt* (Februar 1984): 47.

Ein Schreck,
lich geschicht vnnd gericht
Gottes vber Thomas Mün,
ger, darin Gott offenlich
deſſelbigen geyſt lügen
ſtrafft vnnd ver,
dammet.

Martinus Luther.

Index